D1118712

THE HUNGARIAN REVOLUTION OF 1956 IN RETROSPECT

EDITED BY
BÉLA K. KIRÁLY AND PAUL JÓNÁS

With an Introduction by
G. H. N. Seton-Watson

EAST EUROPEAN QUARTERLY, BOULDER
DISTRIBUTED BY COLUMBIA UNIVERSITY PRESS

1978

EAST EUROPEAN MONOGRAPH SERIES, NO. XL

BROOKLYN COLLEGE
OF
THE CITY UNIVERSITY OF NEW YORK
SCHOOL OF SOCIAL SCIENCE

STUDIES ON SOCIETY IN CHANGE, No. 6

BROOKLYN COLLEGE STUDIES ON
SOCIETY IN CHANGE

—EDITOR IN CHIEF BÉLA K. KIRÁLY—

FOREWORD AND ACKNOWLEDGMENTS

The views expressed in *The Hungarian Revolution of 1956 in Retrospect* do not represent any consensus of beliefs among the editors and contributors. It can be expected that some contributors will not sympathize with all the sentiments expressed here; some may flatly disagree with a few opinions. The editors therefore accept responsibility only for allowing the expressed views to appear in this volume.

The contributions of Anna Kéthly, Tibor Meray and Péter Kende were translated from the Hungarian by Béla K. Király and edited by Peter J. Beales, MA (Cantab.), former managing editor of the monthly *East Europe* (New York). Mr. Beales also edited the text of the rest of the book. The authors wish to express their sincere appreciation to him.

The editors' grateful acknowledgment is also made for the use of excerpts from the following publications:

On Communism: In Defense of the New Course by Imre Nagy. Copyright (C) 1957 by Frederick A. Praeger. Reprinted by permission of Praeger Publishers, a division of Holt, Rinehart and Winston. A reprint of this book was published in 1974 by Greenwood Press, Inc.

"Husz éve" by Anna Kethly, from *Irodalmi Újság*, September-October 1976. Copyright (C) 1976 by Irodalmi Újság (Gazette Littéraire Hongroise). Translated and reprinted by permission.

"Budapest 20 Years Ago" by Béla K. Király, from *The New York Times*, October 23, 1976. Copyright (C) 1976 by The New York Times Company. Reprinted by permission.

Highland Lakes, N. J.
August 20, 1977

Béla K. Király
Paul Jónás

CONTENTS

PREFACE

The publication of this volume on the Hungarian Revolution of 1956 could hardly be more timely. With the passing of two decades since the tumultuous days of that October and November, we can have some confidence now in the historical judgments of a retrospective review. The future is no longer likely to reverse the conclusions of this study that the events which took place in Hungary in 1956 had a significance beyond their time and place. The Hungarian outburst was a segment of universal history: it sprang from the will of a people to free themselves from a system which was both oppressive and foreign. Viewed from this perspective, the Hungarian Revolution must be credited with some great and enduring achievements in spite of its apparent defeat as a political movement.

In another way also, the appearance of this study is well timed. The confluence of events now prominent in world affairs—some probably fortuitous, some possibly inevitable—invite another look at the Hungarian Revolution of 1956. The Helsinki Accord, the Soviet dissident movement, the emergence of Eurocommunism, and President Jimmy Carter's new emphasis on human rights—all have moral and intellectual links with the Hungarian Revolution. The stresses of the modern Russian empire have manifested themselves throughout the world, most clearly in the East Central European countries and, above all, in Hungary. In fact, as this volume makes a point of noting, the Hungarian Revolution was the first instance of a war between socialist states.

Finally, the particular timeliness of this study rests upon the good fortune that it was possible to include the contributions of individuals who participated in the revolution and who also have international reputations for scholarship. This group includes Tamás Aczél and Tibor Méray, leading communist intellectuals; George Heltai, deputy minister of foreign affairs in the revolutionary government; Anna Kéthly, minister of state; Béla Király, major general and chairman of the Revolutionary Council of National Defense; Imre Kovács, secretary general of the National Peasant Party; József Kővágo, secretary general of the Smallholders' Party, and Paul Jónás, president of the Petőfi Circle, the organization of university students.

Other scholars who contributed to the multinational and multi-disciplinary approach of this study include Péter Kende of the University of Paris; Stephen Borsody, formerly of Charles University, Prague; Stephen Fischer-Galaţi of the University of Colorado; George Klein of Western Michigan University; G.H.N. Seton-Watson of the University of London; and Paul E. Zinner of the University of California, Davis.

Some of the papers in this book were presented originally at a November 1976 meeting of the Center for European Studies of the Graduate School of the City University of New York. To the Graduate School and University Center of CUNY we express our appreciation for support and encouragement. Other papers were initially presented at a joint meeting of the American Historical Association and the American Association for the Study of Hungarian History held in Washington, DC, on December 29, 1976. A number of additional papers were commissioned expressly for this publication to insure its balance and comprehensiveness.

The School of Social Science at Brooklyn College is honored to have been a participant in this endeavor.

Nathan Schmukler
Dean, School of Social Science
Brooklyn College

July 11, 1977

INTRODUCTION

The events of 1956 in Hungary remain one of the landmarks of the political memory of my lifetime. I was not there: I only followed the news reports and numerous radio announcements from inside Hungary and from elsewhere, and talked for hours with the Hungarian and foreign friends who had been there and whom I saw in the following weeks, and did my infinitesimal best to awaken my compatriots to the truth and then to help those who had escaped, especially university students. All this was pitifully little; but hardly any event of my lifetime moved me so much. That is why I am glad of this opportunity to make a few observations after twenty years. The fact that they hardly differ from what I wrote at the time is probably proof of my limited understanding or historical imagination; but it may also be an indication that the lessons of those great events were and are so clear that time cannot change them. Nevertheless, time has changed our Western society, and the climate of Western political life, a good deal, so that they bear repeating.

First, let us get the words right. What happened in Hungary was a *revolution*. A revolution is a violent action designed to overthrow a whole system of political and social power and to replace it by something new. Peaceful social transformation, however radical, is *not* a revolution. Violent seizure of power by a clique of politicians or soldiers, designed to grab the existing fruits of power for themselves, is *not* a revolution but a coup d'état (there is still no English word for it). The events in Hungary in the last week of October 1956 were a revolution, in the terms described above. What followed was a *war* between two armies unequal in strength. I will not press this point, as General Béla Király has developed it in his admirable chapter. What followed defeat in war was a *counterrevolution*. This word has unfortunately become a vague term of abuse in the vocabulary of the so-called intellectual left the world over, used to cover any violent action of which these people disapprove. But let us set aside "progressive" pieties and look at reality. A counterrevolution is a violent action designed to overthrow a political and social order established by a revolution and to restore the political and social order that existed before the revolution. This is what happened on November 4, 1956. (One may perhaps argue that the reovlution had not yet created a social order, only a political one, because there had been so little time, but this is a quibble, since the intention to do so is beyond doubt.) Hungary is, tragically, a classic country of counterrevolutions, exceeded in this respect only by France. There were clear cases of counterrevolution in 1849, 1919 and 1956. The agent in the first case was the imperial Russian army of Nicholas I and the beneficiary the Habsburg monarch; in the second case the Rumanian army, and the beneficiary Admiral Miklós Horthy's team; in the third case the discarded leadership of the communist party. However, counterrevolutions in practice never succeed for long in restoring the previous order: the regime of Alexander Bach differed from that of Prince Metternich, the regime of István Bethlen from that of István Tisza, and the regime of János Kádár—Hungarians must with reluctant gratitude acknowledge—from that of Ernő Gerő.

Secondly, the Hungarian Revolution was victorious. It overthrew the Mátyás Rákosi-Ernő Gerő regime. The whole apparently impregnable totalitarian fortress—thought control and personality cult and Moscow worship and all—collapsed in a few days. This was an achievement that nothing can change. Then came the war. The historical parallel and contrast that always occur to me is Poland in 1830: there, too, there was a revolution followed by a war. In 1830-1831 the process lasted ten months, in Hungary twelve days. The reason is not only that the antagonists were more unevenly matched but also that the Soviet army was there, in Hungary, in large numbers and fully armed, when the revolution came. Even so, it retreated, after fierce fighting, and its commanders were told to wait, while the leaders conferred, as Nicholas I had conferred with his advisers, before ordering them to resume the attack.

Thirdly, the question arises why the revolution broke out. The misrule by Soviet agents and the discontent among all classes of the nation were not peculiar only to Hungary, or only to Hungary and Poland: they existed throughout the region of Soviet neocolonialism. However, discontents could only be effective if they found expression within the ruling communist party and this could happen only if a leading personality existed around whom they could polarize. This was possible only in Poland and Hungary, where Władysław Gomułka and Imre Nagy survived: in the other countries of the region the alternative leaders had been done to death in the purges.

Then comes the questions why events took different courses in Poland and in Hungary. Here I must somewhat disagree with my friend Adam Bromke, who expresses the view that has become the conventional wisdom in the West. The difference was not due to the fact that Gomuƚka and Stefan Cardinal Wyszyński were wiser statesmen than Nagy and József Cardinal Mindszenty. They may have been (I am in no position to judge their intimate characters), but events did not depend on them. The two persons who played the decisive role were the outgoing heads of the Stalin-era leadership: Edward Ochab in Poland and Gerő in Hungary. Whereas Ochab accepted the need for change and made a solid front with his successors against Soviet intervention, Gerő refused to yield, and first ordered the AVH (secret police) to shoot on the crowds and then appealed for Soviet intervention. The credit—if credit is due, and if we look at Poland in 1977 I am not so sure that it is—should go not to Gomuƚka but to Ochab; and the blame, if the escalation in Hungary is cause for blame, should go not to Nagy but to Gerő.

Fourthly, I think it is worth stressing that in both Poland and Hungary the aspirations that led to the two crises were not so much nationalist as libertarian and social. What the critics of the Stalin-era regime demanded were civil liberties, impartial justice, economic efficiency and implementation of the social ideas of socialism. It was only when these things were brutally denied, and when a foreign army shot down Hungarian workers and students, that Hungarian national feeling blazed up furiously. I am not, of course, trying to deny that nearly all Hungarians had strong national consciousness and pride in their national traditions. What I do insist on rebutting is the suggestion, endlessly repeated by more or less well-meaning Western "progressives" ever since 1956, that the Revolution was marked by a kind of irresponsible, uncontrollable chauvinism. Quite the contrary is true. It is extraordinary how little was heard of Hungarian national claims on Transylvania or against Czechoslovakia or Yugoslavia: friendship with the neigbouring nations was one of the themes on which the leaders of the Revolution most strongly insisted. It is also quite untrue to suggest that anti-Semitism flared up. It might have been expected, in view of the anti-Semitic passions released by the last pro-Nazi governments of Hungary and in view of the prominence of Hungarian Jews in the communist party. But in fact there was hardly any sign of it—perhaps largely because there were still more Jews among the supporters of Nagy than among the Stalinist rearguard. The attempt to blacken the reputation of the Revolution by insinuations of fascist-type chauvinism and anti-Semitism, understandably pursued by the champions of Soviet policy but unfortunately accepted by honourable Western democrats who should know better, must be resolutely rejected.

One last point should be made about the social forces supporting the Revolution. It is a striking paradox that these were precisely the forces that the Rákosi regime had sought to favour. The young intellectuals who led the first protests consisted precisely of those children of workers and peasants, whose ease of access to higher education (in contrast to the lack of opportunity under the Horthy regime) had been one of the few achievements of which the Rákosi regime had genuine reason to be proud. Events in Hungary showed that, when young people of talent are exposed to modern higher education and modern ideas, they quickly see through ideological obfuscation and the ritual incantations of bureaucrats, grasp the truth and seek ways to act on it. A "toiling intelligentsia" is no less accessible to the infection of truth than a "bourgeois intelligentsia" or a "noble intelligentsia". The same was true, *mutatis mutandis*, of the workers. Floods of rhetoric about the leading role of the working class could not blind Hungarian workers to the fact that they were being overworked and underpaid and in the interests of a new boss class. The rhetoric increased their expectations but did not do away with the evidence of their eyes. It was the workers, the new intellectual elite and the new army that destroyed the totalitarian regime.

* * *

The Hungarian Revolution was not, however, an isolated event: it took place in an international environment. This was disastrously unfavourable to the Hungarians, and fundamentally for reasons that neither they nor anybody else could have prevented. The crisis occurred during the last stages of the campaign for the election of the president of the United States, a four-yearly situation in which demagogy, political dishonesty and cowardice are at a premium. Yet nothing could have been done about this, for the outburst in Hungary which triggered off the Revolution was not planned in advance and the American Constitution cannot be abolished even to help the most deserving cause The crisis also coincided with the Suez crisis. This was the culmination of a long series of events and the result of planning between the British, French and Israeli governments (misguided or immoral, perhaps), which could not suddenly be called off. That Hungarians should have felt at the time that the western Powers shamelessly and cynically exploited their heroism to grab something for themselves, is psychologically understandable, but this view is not supported by the facts; nor is the view, loudly proclaimed and possibly genuinely believed at the time by Soviet propagandists, that the revolt of the Hungarians and the attack on Egypt were two prongs of a double offensive by "imperialism" against the forces of "socialism and peace". The results were disastrous for Hungary. Not only was it clear that the British and French had no thoughts for anything but their Egyptian enterprise but also the savage attack by American Secretary of State John Foster Dulles on the British and French leaders (whom a few months earlier he had urged to stand up to Egyptian President Gamal Abdel Nasser) was clear proof of schism in the Western camp. It gave the green light for the Soviet invasion of Hungary.

The appeal by Nagy to the United Nations to protect a neutralized Hungary was not, as so often stated in the West, a foolish gesture of provocation. On the contrary, as the contributions of Dr. Kővágó and Dr. Heltai to this volume very clearly show, it was a last desperate attempt to save Hungary. It was not at all foolish. It was only a year since the Soviet Union had agreed to the neutralization of Austria, codified in the *Staatsvertrag* signed by the four Powers. Moreover, with a neutral state on its western border, Hungary was strategically in a much less sensitive position than Czechoslovakia or Poland. A further point worth remembering is that the whole political development in Hungary during the twelve days of the Revolution was toward a grouping around a large democratic socialist party (including elements from the communist party) and a large democratic party with Catholic and peasant influences—the same grouping as existed in Austria.

It may, of course, be argued that this in no way diminishes the Soviet government's reasons to wish to invade: it was not the prospect of Hungary's being neutral but the prospect of formerly communist-ruled Hungary becoming a state of multiparty democracy that aroused implacable Soviet hostility. This is also my own view and was my view at the time. I would further argue that events in Czechoslovakia in 1968 confirm this hypothesis. The Czechoslovaks took care not formally to introduce a multiparty regime but they were in fact allowing their communist party to turn itself into a social democratic party in all but name, which is almost the same thing—or, for a Moscow communist, perhaps even worse.

But there is more to be said. Contributors to this book rightly emphasize that there was no contingency planning on the Western, especially American, side for revolution in an East Central European state and that the diplomatic representatives of the Western allies had virtually no contact with the Nagy government. We must ask ourselves the question: Could nothing have been done? I have spent many hours in the last twenty years discussing this with British and American diplomats, journalists and even a few politicians; and all have insisted that nothing could have been done. And yet I confess that I am not convinced. Of course, American military invasion of Hungary was not possible, still less a nuclear ultimatum to Moscow. Of course, formal diplomatic notes could achieve nothing. But was it really impossible for the United States government, using all the private and public channels of communication available to it and all the means of pressure at its disposal, to have convinced the Soviet government that the consequences of invasion would have been very much more unpleasant for it than the consequences of letting the Nagy government, *which was in control of Hungary*, stay in power until a settlement, acceptable to all parties concerned, including the Great Powers, could be worked out? The truth is that the United States government did not even try. Dulles revealed himself an empty demagogue. Nobody tried because everyone was obsessed with the presidential election and the Suez Canal. The same indifference was displayed in 1968 toward Czechoslovakia. Once more there was a presidential election in prospect and instead of Egypt there was Vietnam. The fact that they had got away with invading Hungary gave good grounds for the Soviet leaders to believe that they would get away with Czechoslovakia too.

Did the Soviet Union gain or lose from its action? The optimist will say that it lost, since Soviet brutality was exposed to the world and numerous intellectuals of the left abandoned the official communist movement. This is undoubtedly true. It is, however, also true that it gained as well, since it showed that no Western state would stand up to its aggression. The Romans used to say of their subjects: *oderint dum metuant*. Whether this will always be true depends not on the Soviet leaders but on the leaders of the United States and to some extent also of other Western nations.

It is rightly pointed out by one of our contributors that Imre Nagy was a sort of proto-Eurocommunist, a man who believed in a socialism that would respect Western liberties and fit into European culture. In many Western communist parties today there are men and women who share this outlook; it is reflected in the public speeches of Western communist leaders; and it appeals strongly to nonparty Westerners who may decide to give their votes to communist parties. But before we congratulate ourselves on the acceptance by the Western communist parties of Imre Nagy's political legacy, let us not forget another legacy from Hungarian communism.

In 1946 Rákosi himself talked irreproachably democratic language and his *faux bonhomme* manner impressed many visiting Western journalists. But it was he whose "salami tactics", applied not (Heaven forbid) to democratic conservative or liberal parties but only to "fascist" or "counterrevolutionary" fringes of such parties, gradually reduced his coalition partners to empty shells.

Can American and other Western leaders learn these lessons? Can they find ways of persuading the Soviet leaders that it is *not to their own interest* to go on subjecting their dependent nations to national humiliation? Can they find a way of showing them that the Finlandization of Eastern Europe will increase the security of the Soviet Union? Or shall we see a process first of Finlandization and then of Polonization of Western Europe? The answers to these questions depend not only on the degree of aggressive self-confidence in Moscow but also on the political perception and willpower in Washington: the first is largely shaped by the second.

The Hungarian Revolution has scored two achievements already. It showed the world that totalitarianism could be overthrown. It won even from its conquerors respect which has been reflected in more humane conditions than exist anywhere in the Soviet empire. The third possible achievement, the opening of Western eyes once and for all to the unpleasant realities of an ever more dangerous world, has still not been attained.

Imre Nagy

ETHICS AND MORALS IN HUNGARIAN PUBLIC LIFE
(Excerpts)

What are the symptoms of the current ethical and moral crisis in society and Party life?

. . . The lofty ideals and principles of socialism, which have great appeal to a large sector of the people in our country, are increasingly losing their true significance in the public consciousness due to the people's experiences in their everyday life, their social life, and their working conditions since the liquidation of the June policy.* The violent contrast between words and deeds, between principles and their realization, is rocking the foundations of our people's democracy, our society, and our Party. This contrast, of which the people are becoming more and more aware, is leading to dissension and to loss of faith among the masses, who hope for a better, happier, and more peaceful life, and for the realization of the truly high ideals of socialism. The working people are unable to reconcile the rapid progress of socialism with the deterioration, or at least stagnation, of their standard of living. The people cannot understand how it is that, the greater the results they achieve in the economic, political, social, or cultural field, the greater their burdens become. They feel more and more that the immeasurable sacrifices they have made in working harder or accepting a lower standard of living are not commensurate to the results achieved. They are beginning to doubt ever more seriously whether this road, which consumes all their work and most of their material and spiritual wealth without bringing them any closer to the fulfillment of their hopes through the attainment of socialist ideals, is indeed the true road to socialism. These doubts are entertained not only by the petty bourgeoisie or by vacillating intellectuals, but by the working masses, and this means an increasing renunciation of socialism. Not only the non-Party, untrained working masses are involved. Party members, even Party old-timers, are frequently voicing their misgivings about the faulty policies of the leadership and the impermissible, antisocialist methods and devices that have been used to implement these policies. And their answers are ever more frequently and emphatically a denial of present methods. This doubt, this loss of faith in the ideal, this compromising of socialism through the mistaken

---

* The program known as the "New Course," which Imre Nagy promulgated in June, 1953, after installation as chairman of the Council of Ministers (prime minister).

policy of the Party leadership, is a consequence of the stupid and harmful political recklessness that was a result of the March resolution.[†] The paths, methods, devices, and forms of socialism that the Party leadership is attempting to force upon the members, and to present with their help as a desirable goal to the workers and the government, are receiving less and less support from the masses. This is because these paths to socialism and these methods ignore man, the greatest asset, with his many desires and needs, all of which demand a standard of living higher than was attainable under the preceding capitalist system. The Hungarian people reject the old system and its masters, and they will crush all attempts to bring it back, no matter in what form. The Hungarian working people, who made many sacrifices in the struggle against the old system and for the establishment of the new socialist system, do not desire to risk or bargain away the fruits of their victory, but want to increase them. They want to follow that path to socialism which is better, easier, more tolerable and humane, and more in keeping with Hungarian conditions, circumstances, potentialities, and traditions; they desire to follow the path of development set forth by the June resolution and the policy of the New Course, rather than that catastrophic policy which has already bankrupted the country once, compromised the ideals of socialism, and proved that its goals and tasks were untenable. Fear of a repetition of this is giving rise to serious doubts among Party members and the working masses. Furthermore, the danger of a repetition has been growing and becoming ever more pronounced since the March resolution and the subsequent Party resolutions. The policy of insistence on the March "principles" has become a tension-creating, undermining force which is as destructive to our economic and political life, to the basis of our society, and to our official morals and policies as the political goals, the humanism, the superior moral and ethical purity of June and of the New Course were creative. In their blindness, the leaders fail to consider public opinion; they do not realize what a powerful political and moral factor it has become; and they either do not see or prefer to ignore the fact that the public opinion of the nation is increasingly condemning and turning against the activities of the Party and the government. Let them realize at last the consequences of making an empty phrase of the slogan: "With the people, for the people, through thick and thin." In the interests of the people, the country, and socialism, let them depend not on bayonets but on the people.

The danger of the Party leadership's policy, which serves personal dictatorship, lies in the fact that it attempts to frighten Party members and the masses away from the June policy by predicting that the June

---

[†] The Central Committee resolution of March 4, 1955, that denounced "right-wing" and "opportunist deviation" under the New Course and Imre Nagy for encouraging it by his "anti-Marxist views." It ordered renewed emphasis on heavy industry and "consolidation and enlargement of the kolkhoz movement." Six weeks later, on April 14, 1955, Nagy was dismissed as prime minister and expelled from the Politburo and Central Committee.

the aid of the AVH, which became predominant in the Party—forced it to execute his wishes.

Bonapartism, individual dictatorship, and the employment of force did not become predominant in state and Party life automatically. In this field, serious responsibility rests on the policy of Stalin, which gave far-reaching aid to the liquidation of anti-Bonapartist forces inside and outside the Party. Without this aid, depending merely on his own power and influence, Rákosi would have been unable to achieve individual dictatorship. To bring about the triumph of Bonapartism, the allies of socialist democracy had to be destroyed. To bring about individual dictatorship, the Party's leading cadres had to be exterminated and the AVH had to be made the supreme power so that it could carry out assigned tasks. This is all historical fact. Such degeneration of power and of Party life inevitably sweeps the nation and Party toward catastrophe. The June resolution of the Central Committee and the policy of the New Course were required in state and Party life alike to avert this danger. In the life of the state, their principal task was the elimination of Bonapartism, the consolidation of the power of the working class, the assurance of its leadership role, and the revival of local councils and the People's Front through the development of a worker-peasant alliance. Validity had to be obtained for the rights and responsibilities of citizens and men as established in the Constitution; shaken law and order had to be consolidated; legality had to be restored; the role of the state had to be clarified; and the relationship of the state and Party had to be put on a new basis. In the interest of putting an end to personal dictatorship and the elimination of führerism, the following tasks had to be undertaken: the development of collective leadership in the Party; the development of criticism and self-criticism for assuring democracy within the Party; the restoration of the Party membership's rights as assured by the organizational laws; and the restoration and further development of the Party's prestige and its influence upon the masses. series of blows inflicted upon Bonapartism and personal dictatorship after the resolution of June, 1953, are of immense significance for our future development and for the fate of socialism. During the period of the New Course, powerful moral forces were unleashed, which could not be suppressed by the March resolutions of the Party, by subsequent resolutions, or by terroristic methods. However, these moral forces were unable to prevent the return of Bonapartism and personal dictatorship in 1955 . . . .

This Machiavellianism, which is in conflict not only with socialism but with all the moral principles of progressive mankind, is gaining more and more ground in our government and in our social and Party life. Thus it can happen that although we have a constitution, a legal system, and laws that should ensure our socialist development, these things become mere devices for personal dictatorship over most of the people in the hands of the Bonapartist power.

The belief in socialist legality and in legality itself has been shaken. The abuse of power and the use of illegal devices reached alarming proportions in 1955 and exceeded even the malpractices of the period from 1950 to 1952. The situation has degenerated to such an extent that most of the workers have come to believe that they are at the mercy of illegalities and abuses, and that there are no laws that protect their rights as human beings and citizens. A striking and potentially dangerous consequence of the degeneration of power and the alienation of the people is the spread of the theory that a People's Democracy is synonymous with anarchy; that such a democracy leaves plenty of room for illegalities; that in such a democracy the life of the individual is characterized by constant insecurity and fear. The June 1953 resolution of the Central Committee classified the violation of legality that it exposed as serious and dangerous, but the situation had not degenerated then to the extent that it has today.

The government and the Party leadership ignore completely the traditional or instinctive sense of justice of the masses, which developed in harmony with social morals. The legislature is insensitive in this regard also, while the enforcement of the laws and the execution of justice violate it crudely in every way. The administration of justice, which as a consequence of the degeneration of power cannot carry out the principle of socialist legality amid the conditions of Bonapartist dictatorship, is being crushed between the people and the rule; it is increasingly moving away from its moral and ethical moorings in the People's Democratic system, and from the people's sense of justice and feeling for Socialist legality; whereas, in the triumph of Socialism, as in all progressive social concepts, justice must play an exceptionally significant role, which together with the struggle of the working masses and everyday constructive work turns into a powerful material force indispensable to the establishment of socialist society. The judiciary must serve this social justice—this socialist social justice in our case—and the legal dictatorship, which is separated from the working class and masses, is utilizing the administration of justice to serve its own assaults against the people. The degeneration of power and the moral crisis of social life are also evidenced by the fact that at present the number of persons imprisoned is greater than ever before; the number of those sentenced exceeds those imprisoned to such an extent that many thousands cannot begin to serve their sentence because of a lack of "space." But the most alarming fact is that the majority of those convicted have come from the ranks of the working class, the industrial workers. This, more than anything else, is evidence of the degeneration of power and economic and social conditions under which the working class is carrying on its task of socialist construction, and of the moral and ethical crisis that was brought about by these conditions.

Public morality is an indispensable requirement of socialist society.... It is not compatible with public morality to have in positions of leadership the directors and organizers of mass lawsuits, or those responsible for the torturing and killing of innocent people, or organizers of international provocations, or economic saboteurs, or squanderers of public property who, through the abuse of power, either have committed serious crimes against the people or are forcing others to commit these crimes. The public, the Party, and the state organs must be cleansed of these elements. . . .

What sort of political morality is there in a public life where contrary opinions are not only suppressed but punished with actual deprivation of livelihood; where those who express contrary opinions are expelled from society with shameful disregard for the human and civil rights set down in the Constitution; where those who are opposed in principle to the ruling political trend are barred from their professions—the journalist from his work in the area of the press, the author from his literary activities; and where a man is not only dismissed from his political office but from membership in the Hungarian Academy of Sciences and from his university teaching position as well; and indeed where all those activities whereby he might guarantee his livelihood are made impossible for him? What is this if not a shameful degeneration of political morality? Can one speak, in such a case, of a Constitution, of law and order, of legality; can one speak of the morality of public life when the "battle of opinions" is waged with such depraved tools, when they lie about freedom and at the same time deprive the brave representatives of freedom of the bare necessities of life? This is not socialist morality. Rather it is modern Machiavellianism.

This all-powerful material dependence, this anxiety for bread, is killing the most noble human virtues, virtues that should most especially be developed in a socialist society: courage, resolution, sincerity and frankness, consistency of principle, and strength. In their place, the leaders have made virtues of self-abasement, cowardice, hypocrisy, lack of principle, and lies. The degeneration and corruption of public life and the deterioration of character that takes place in society as a result thereof are among the most serious manifestations of the moral-ethical crisis that is taking place before our eyes. We must also see, however, that the deterioration of public life and of character has repercussions in every area of our social life, and that it hastens the decay brought on by the ever intensifying economic and political crisis. Falsehood and careerism are spreading dangerously in our public life and are deeply affecting human morality and honor; distrust is gaining ground; and an atmosphere of suspicion and revenge is banishing the fundamental feature of socialist morality, humanism; in its stead, cold inhumanity is appearing in public life. It is a shocking picture that the moral situation of our social life reveals.

The picture is no better in the Party or with regard to Communist morality. The weakness of Party morals is apparent from the trials, the rehabilitations, that have taken place, which reveal the degeneration of Party morality. The organs of the Party leadership have pronounced judgments that condemn not the criminals but their victims. Whatever has become of Communist morality, human respect, and honor, if there are Communist leaders according to whom the unjustly executed Comrade László Rajk was a coward because he admitted to false charges in order to deceive the Party leaders, leaders who act as if it were not they themselves who contrived the mendacious charges and the means for getting the confession? . . .

Why do they outrage the memory of the deceased Rajk, and why do they protect and conceal the real criminals who are well known by name, i.e., the members of the clique, the so-called "foursome," Rákosi,

Farkas, Gerő, and Révai?* Is this considered compatible with Communist morality, with human honor and dignity? They do it in the interest of Party unity—as they keep saying—but they forget that the Party is not a den of criminals, whose unity must be preserved by hiding their crimes. What kind of unity is it that is held together by knowledge of and participation in crime? Their answer is that "we do not moralize," and that this is a political question and not a moral one. They do not perceive that they have thereby condemned their policies and have admitted the loss of all moral ground. . . . .

What kind of Communist morality is it in the name of which they now denounce László Rajk because, according to them, he confessed to the false charges raised against him because he was too cowardly to reject them, when in the name of this same Communist morality, the Central Committee condemned and expelled me from the Party because I was unwilling to assume responsibility for the false charge raised against me? What sort of political morality prevails in the leadership of the Party, where the truth is measured and Communist behavior assessed in such a manner? The foregoing, however, are only flagrant examples, only certain crude cases, of the deterioration of Communist morality. Much more perilous are the similar, all-too-prevalent occurrences that are spreading among Party officials and throughout Party ranks. As the dictatorship of the proletariat, because of the degeneration of its power into Bonapartism and personal dictatorship, is gradually losing its broad democratism, and raw power and reprisal are used more and more not only against hostile, reactionary, antipopular forces but also against the broad masses of the working people, similarly the Bonapartist spirit, personal dictatorship, regimentation, and slavish subordination are supplanting Party democracy, democratic centralism, and Leninist theories of Party life. In this atmosphere and confronted with such methods and means, Party life, debate, the exchange of ideas, and the cleansing of ideological deviations through the free battle of opinions, without which unity of principle in the Party cannot be created, are dying out. Among Party members, it kills initiative, spontaneous activity, and enthusiasm, which are being replaced by apathy and unconcern. The rapid spread of Bonapartism, of personal dictatorship, is destroying Leninist Party life. The liquidation of Party democracy and the introduction of dictatorship inevitably are accompanied by the dictatorial methods and techniques that have prevailed in the Party for the past six months. Intimidation and terror, insinuation and baseless charges, and the denunciation and branding of others as enemies have become mass method. They are the crux of the moral crisis in Party life. . . .

Another characteristic symptom of the deterioration of morality in public life, a symptom that has become actually epidemic in social and Party life, is careerism, the pushing and elbowing for favors, even alms, from above. If this were simply a remnant from the past, it would be

---

*Four Politburo members: Mátyás Rákosi, Mihály Farkas, Ernő Gerő and József Révai.

NAGY ON ETHICS AND MORALS 17

easier to exterminate. Unfortunately, this is not simply a question of remnants from the past, but derives from the stifling of criticism, the intimidation, and the retaliation against candid speech that are in evidence now in the leadership and that unavoidably lead to the spread of opportunism. The careerists are sycophants, bootlickers; they have no principles or opinions of their own and will say without any compunction that black is white. In every case, they seek the favor of those who are in a position to assure them a better place in Party or state affairs, greater prestige, more income, broader authority, and, last but not least, a limousine. They go to any length to gain the favor of the leaders; they grovel and bow and scrape before them; they flatter them. The deterioration of morality in public life pleases the careerists, whom, unfortunately, we may encounter on all sides. The number of them tends to increase because, instead of denouncing them, the leaders tolerate and quite frequently even pamper them, since their kowtowing flatters the vanity of the leaders, as they will do anything or carry out any orders for them without reservation.

Opportunism is not an individual character deficiency but first and foremost a social symptom, which is found where an individual's position in society is determined not by his performance or ability but by those traits with which we have characterized the opportunist above . . . .

We have two ways in which to extricate ourselves from the disastrous situation brought upon the country by the Rákosi regime: we can either liquidate Stalinist policy ourselves in good time and lead the country back to the June road, by which we shall be able to avoid economic and political failure; or we can refrain from changing the course of events with the result that the increasing tension may bring the country to the verge of a grave crisis. . . .

(December 1955)

TWENTY YEARS AGO

I still have vivid recollections of the events of twenty years ago. It is rather as though barely a couple of years have passed. I am quite certain that at that time my compatriots, like myself, believed we were on the threshold of a new, happier, safer world. We felt we had in our hands all the means to transform our country and lay the foundations of a secure existence. Not only were we filled with *hope* but also with the *conviction* that we could stand on our own feet, shape our destiny according to our own needs and take the place we deserved in the European community of nations. Imre Nagy sent me on a mission to Vienna to secure the support of the Socialist International, which was meeting there, with no *thought in the back of his mind* of detaching Hungary from the Soviet Union, but he did think—and so did the whole country—that we would serve our country's independence better if we did not bind ourselves to one side alone but remained neutral toward every side. It is fateful and dangerous for small nations to be enmeshed in the sphere of interest of *one* great power and to have to serve that power's interests. This effort was brought to naught by the intervention of hastily sent-in Soviet troops. We were well aware already that Hungary had not regained real independence at the end of the [Second World] War and that the occupiers would intervene in the course of the Revolution even if there had not been domestic forces with good reason to fear lest a successful revolution bring them to book for their machinations thitherto. In this regard, the sole comfort has been that the Soviet Union itself realized that those it had imposed on Hungary were jeopardizing even its own interests. It quickly changed their policies and recalled or ousted those who had done more harm than good to the power that was to remain firmly in occupation.

The Revolution failed in its goals, it did not win us self-determination, but at least it swept away those who were not serving the Hungarian people's interests. Afraid for their skins, some of the kinglets were forced into exile anew and some retired into domestic exile where they bemoan their long-bygone powers. Yet ever since we have known that the new proxies, though using different methods, are doing the same as the former proconsuls. Suffice it perhaps to mention as a watchword the name of *Záhony*, that small town in northern Hungary through which the lifeblood of the Hungarian people is pouring as from a severed vein. I recently read an account of *Záhony*'s importance—I was astonished this article could even be published [in Hungary] : it reported that the *Záhony* transshipping yards have been extended *several kilometers*. To insure transshipping goes on nonstop, even expectant mothers are put to work. There are hardly any statistics on Hungarian consumption but we often read about "shortages of goods" and wonder why, despite the fact exports to the West are going down, the goods left in the country are always scarce. We know that there are often complaints, which have even been published in the press. These complaints have recently been stopped. The need to earn foreign exchange is what inspires exports to the West but little publicity or explanation is offered for exports to the East.

The vast Soviet Union, spreading over two continents, has an interest in imports coming from Hungary. Its Asian and European territories would be capable of every kind of industrial and agricultural achievement if the right people were working at the right jobs. The example of the United States—not to mention anywhere else— ought to be an inducement to its whole productive apparatus. But man is the instrument and object of production; if the man who tills the soil does not see the need to produce *in excess of his own requirements* to supply those who will be providing him with manufactured goods in exchange, then economic designs lose their meaning. An undemanding rural population does not seek manufactured supplies. Those in power—those seen to be from a distance—are making no effort to stimulate demand. Consumer demand of the European type has not formed in the immense territory stretching from the German border in Europe to the Chinese border. The needs of the European "island-city" of Moscow are supplied by the European satellites. This, then, is the purpose of Hungary's exports—except that those to the West earn foreign exchange.

Fulfilling his obligations to the Holy Alliance, Tsar Nicholas I in 1848-49 readily sped to the assistance of a hard-pressed fellow monarch. In the hour of peril [Sándor] Petőfi sounded the alarm: "The Russians are coming, the Russians are coming." The invading Russians reached the Hungarian capital; contemporary newspapers show Ivans and Sergeis in the National Museum getting drunk on the alcohol for preserving specimens. Things have changed since then; during the days of the revolution we saw the Russians making ready to withdraw, acting in a truly European fashion, filled with understanding and sympathy for the Hungarian revolution. Though some of them—primarily the newly deployed troops—thought they had arrived at the Suez Canal, most of them—particularly those who had been stationed near Hungarian towns till then—knew that the Hungarian people had begun fighting for the chance to make a livelihood and for the preservation of their national existence. We do not know what happened to them, whether they were banished to remote northern, Asian areas or whether they were summarily dealt with in a more effective way than lengthy reeducation.

Hungary's destiny has been turned about again; back have come Moscow's pathfinders who, in return for privileges offered, have undertaken to drive the notion of revolution out of the Hungarian people's minds. What survives from the 1956 revolution recalls a dispatch from the past. In 1849, after completing his mission on behalf of the Holy Alliance, the commander in chief of the Russian army of invasion reported his success to his powerful master with the words: "Hungary lies at Your Majesty's feet." The powers that hold sway over today's Hungary could make the same report: Hungary lies at the feet of the red tsars, twenty years after the slaying of the revolution.

PART I
DOMESTIC ASPECTS OF THE HUNGARIAN REVOLUTION

INTELLECTUAL ASPECTS

The Hungarian communist party's preoccupation with writers and intellectuals concealed behind the mask of paternal solicitude a fundamental fear and contempt for them. Ostensibly, the leaders of the Party considered it their duty "to keep an eye" on the intellectuals and, if necessary, "to protect" them, like children, mainly from themselves, lest they fall and bump their heads. In reality, however, the abnormal, clearly paranoid concern of the party leaders revealed a keen awareness of the traditional role of writers and intellectuals not only in Hungary but also in Eastern Europe in general, as implacable enemies of oppression, colonization, tyranny. The strategy of the party in relation to its intellectuals has been determined by a set of interrelated problems, geographical, religious, historical, political, which were instrumental in forming the archetypal patterns and social consciousness of the people of Eastern Europe, and of Hungary in particular.

Geographically Hungary is a landlocked country without a single outlet to warm seas, ship-swaying currents, challenging oceans. The result has been an outward-longing but inward-looking culture and literature which in its long history could never altogether manage to purge itself from the stigma of provinciality. Sir Francis Drake set out to sail around the world. About the same time, Baron Bálint Balassi set out from Hungary to Kraków. Sir Francis was lured by the glitter of the unknown, its famed treasures and treasured fame; the baron, perhaps, by some dubious beauties of certain houses of ill repute on Castle [Grodzka] Street or, conceivably, by the masterly Renaissance chapel of Bartolommeo Berecci. Behind Drake's flapping sails there remained a strong queen and a vigorous country; behind Balassi's tired steed, a lovelorn mistress and a Hungary about to be buried under the tidal wave of the sultan's janissaries. To his merit, though, he was quite conscious of his country's future as well as his moral, spiritual—and military—commitments. "Farewell," he opened his great valedictory poem, "Farewell, my sweet homeland, good Hungary, shield of Christianity." He returned, five years later, to try to save his sweet *patria* and died in battle, shielding Christianity on the walls of the archbishopric of Esztergom. The tone as well as the pattern was set.

By then, of course, Christianity had long become both the spiritual wellspring and the intellectual mode of Eastern Europe, though Christianity itself was already fighting its bloody and interminable war over the gist of authority, the gift of grace and the glory of God. The conflict between the elegant antiquity, urbane optimism and refined traditionalism of Roman Catholicism and the rebellious spirit, stern solemnity and artless gravity of Protestantism created the foundation of modern nations, cultures and literatures. Meanwhile, the transcendental-archetypal content of old religions of transfixed shamans, ritual sacrifices and violent cosmogonies was absorbed by the stronger and more purposeful spirituality of Christianity, yet it survived, part folklore, part superstition, in the tales of images of death and rebirth, heaven and earth, sun and moon, as sacred trees, stones, flowers of some primordial revelation. Together they formed a healthy and viable folk spirituality and religiosity which were one of the essential elements in the fight of the Hungarians for survival.

Historically, Hungary was a country whose development was interrupted and for centuries delayed by foreign occupations, which threatened the very existence of its people under the oppressive forces of alien customs, foreign methods, strange religions. The English had their bloody disagreements with the French or the Spanish, and popes and emperors did not become famous for their reticence in sending their vassals, mercenaries, peasant foot soldiers to battle for their rights of investiture. Yet their peoples, though they suffered long and hard, had never faced an immediate prospect of total annihilation, extinction, absorption by alien political and cultural systems. The Poles, Hungarians, Serbs, Macedonians, Bulgarians did, and more than once in their history: the waves of Tartars, Turks, Germans, Austrians, Russians played havoc not only with their villages, vineyards and virgins, but also with the very fabric of their existence. The result of this "cardiac arrest" of natural economic and political growth was that the industrial and political revolutions of the eighteenth and nineteenth centuries could not take place, were aborted or defeated, while the feudal organization of land, society and wealth survived until almost the end of the nineteenth century and its vestiges even long afterward.

It was mainly for these reasons that the idea of "nation" assumed, in the course of Hungarian history, quasi-mythical dimensions both in politics and literature, despite the ever widening rift between ruler and ruled, folk nation and political state, and the idea of the "poet" assumed even more pronounced mythical, well-nigh "prophetic" powers and proportions. In this mythical world of people and poets, "nation" was identified consistently with the myth-creating peasantry and came to imply moral goodness and virtue. More importantly, perhaps, it meant not only a community of men and women with common history, language, customs, unconscious memories of prehistoric landscapes, fires, frights and fights, but also the idea of ethnic, religious and political survival. So, when the poets assailed or lamented the faults and shortcomings of the "nation" or sang its praises, they assumed the role of tribal shamans, Biblical prophets and opposition politicians. In short, they became gradually central, if often powerless, characters in the historical drama and created an intensely national—often nationalistic—literature whose commitment to the primacy of the nation—their sweet *patria*—was at once mythological, political and personal.

No wonder that even the first tentative stirrings of Hungarian writers and intellectuals in 1953 (at the time of the first government of Imre Nagy) were viewed with suspicion, distrust and—no doubt—hostility. Strangely, the world was about to turn upside down: everything that had been emphasized as "historical tradition" was being transformed into a "historical presence," much more menacing than the (real or imaginary) class enemies. Within a few weeks in the summer of 1953, the writers became the prime target of attack and, in an as yet undetermined fashion, the main enemies of the ruling bureaucracy. The reform movement of the intellectuals was aimed at restoring the historical balance between oppressive forces and prophetic powers and, however tentatively, attempted to recreate the historical pattern of the writer's role in the social and political development of the country. Old political and historical "sympathies" were revived between the Poles and the Hungarians, yet the appearance of a genuine "internationalism" did not, in this instance, meet with the approval of the internationalist party. What was even worse, by the summer of 1956, not only did many Poles, themselves in the throes of great moral and political transformation, support openly the fight of the Hungarian intellectuals, but also even a small number of Russian intellectuals had managed to send encouraging messages through sundry Hungarian intermediaries, such as students, tourists or delegation members, returning from the USSR during the turbulent weeks of October-November 1956. I remember the message, hastily scribbled on the back of a matchbox by the late Emmanuel Kazakevich, a distinguished Leningrad writer and Stalin Prize winner, to the Hungarian writers: "If you win your battle in Hungary, perhaps we in the Soviet Union will win our war." Here might be the beginnings of the Russian intellectual movement that a decade later had become a serious moral and political force in the Soviet Union, the target of persecution and oppression, yet also the source of resistance.

In any case, the Hungarian party was always ready to fight against the emerging movement of the writers and intellectuals—at first with the usual methods of bribery and blackmail and later with more lethal weapons. I remember an occasion in 1955 when Mátyás Rákosi summoned me to his office for a little "chitchat." It was just after a long and stormy session of the Politburo at which it had become apparent that blackmail and bribery and intimidation had failed and that the split between the writers and the party leaders was open and probably irrevocable. I stood there before his desk, filled with dark forebodings. He looked old, exhausted, flabbergasted, altogether incapable of comprehending what had happened. After a brief pause he said: "What do you want? Tell me, what do you really want? Haven't we given you everything? Tell me." Clearly, if I had said I wanted a new apartment or a new car or a trip to New York, my wish would have been granted immediately. That was the way his mind worked. Also his politics.

These tactics, of course, were not unique to Rákosi. In Czechoslovakia Antonín Novotný applied the same pressures, feeling the same way about intellectuals in general and writers in particular. "The writer should be held in the palm of one's hand like a sparrow," he was reported to have told to Eduard Goldstücker, then president of the Czechoslovak Writers' Union. "You must not squeeze him too hard or he might die, yet you mustn't open your palm or he will fly away. What you have to do is pluck out his feathers one by one. Then, even if he flies away, he will always return to the warmth of your hand."

However, by the time the revolt of the writers had intensified and the party felt threatened by the sparrow's misbehavior, the warm poetic metaphors had disappeared and the general attitude was beginning to freeze. In August 1956, János Kádár called a conference at party headquarters to discuss the writers' "antiparty" movement, this time comparing them to "flies." Just out of jail and recently reinstated as a member of the Politburo, Kádár told us: "You [the writers] believe that you alone are responsible for the changes that took place in July [Rákosi's fall]. You had better understand once and for all that these changes were directed by the Central Committee and carried out by our ordinary workers and peasants. The writers remind me of the fly that settles on the reins and thinks he pulls the cart."

His sarcasm and his undisguised fury expressed for us the party's subconscious terror of anything it had not accomplished by itself, that came from without—outside its ideological, political and police boundaries—yet it represented a viable alternative, a trend, an idea running counter to its dogmata and directives. But by then it was too late.

The sense of freedom, of moral and intellectual rebirth, was overwhelmingly accepted as the main source of the intellectual movement. It generated an atmosphere that captured the imagination of the people and reactivated latent national energies. The emphasis on moral renewal, however, did not mean that the movement ignored the country's very real economic difficulties. As far back as 1953, Hungarian intellectuals had protested the workers' and peasants' low standard of living and a deep awareness of these economic weaknesses had lent a greater urgency to their quest for moral change. Yet their protest was not based on classic Marxist economic arguments. Even when the problem of Soviet economic exploitation was publicly aired in the case of uranium ore, the emphasis was clearly on the moral rather than the economic or even political aspects of the issue. Professor Lajos Jánosi said at the meeting of the Petőfi Circle in Budapest on June 27, 1956: "Recently, when we went to Moscow to confer with our Soviet colleagues, it turned out they knew considerably more about Hungarian uranium fields than we did. This is a morally indefensible situation."

The intellectual community's preoccupation with the moral aspects of the situation was hardly accidental. The leaders of the intellectual revolt were, almost without exception, party members, members of the new class, many of whom recognized their personal, if unwilling, complicity in the crimes of the past.

In A Letter to My Friends the novelist Tibor Déry wrote: "During the last ten years our country has been pulled inch by inch from under our feet. We thought we were going to build socialism; instead, they put us behind prison walls build of blood and lies. I myself feel responsible because my eyes were opened late, and when

they were, I found that neither my voice nor my silence were elo-
quent to communicate to all." Or as the poet László Benjamin put it
when a friend, innocently arrested and imprisoned for five years,
suddenly returned from the "nothingness" of the terror: "It is my
crime to have believed in yours!"

Disillusioned, sharing a deep sense of guilt, the intellectuals turned to the future. Their first task was to clarify the distinction between the truth of the party and what a Czechoslovak philosopher
labeled twelve years later "the fundamental truth." Miklós Gimes,
once editor of *Szabad Nép* [Free People], the party's official daily,
later executed for his participation in the revolution as a close friend
and adviser to Prime Minister Imre Nagy, wrote: "We have been told
that there are two kinds of truths, that the truth of the party can be
more important than objective truth. We have been taught that the
truth and political expediency are in fact identical . . . . If there is a
truth of a higher order than objective truth, if the single criterion of
truth is political expediency, then even a lie can be 'true,' for even a
lie can be momentarily expedient. This is a terrible thought, yet its
importance must be squarely faced."

Here was the essential difference between the new and the old
morality; between the party, for which reforms and changes were
only a matter of expediency—political tactics, and the communist
intellectuals, who had now recognized the lie within the truth. The
chasm, of course, that divided the party's contemporary nihilists,
the *apparatchiki* for whom truth and lie were interchangeable, from
the communist intellectuals, whose devotion to the transformation
of society was genuine and sincere, had always been there. But this
was the moment when it emerged into the open fully and inevitably.
Indeed, the communist bureaucracy became the principal object of
the wrath and moral indignation of the awakening intellectuals. In
his now famous satirical essay, "Why I Dislike Comrade Kucsera",
the playwright Gyula Háy wrote: "Kucsera is an upstart and all
parvenus, like the *nouveaux riches* who give themselves airs because
of their newly acquired wealth, are repulsive. I doubt whether history has ever known a comparable flourishing of *parvenus* like the
Kucseras . . . . Kucsera with his salary, car, apartment, private shops
and rest houses each day grows more and more alienated from the
people, from the party. . . . The other reason why I dislike Comrade
Kucsera is his dilettantism. Kucsera knows nothing and meddles in
everything."

The *apparatchik*'s moral and political weaknesses had now been
exposed. Háy continued: "Lies are not lies for Kucsera, murder is

not murder, justice is not justice, and man is not man. Kucsera preaches 'socialism' and means a system that, hindering socialist progress, keeps him going. He preaches 'unity' and applies it to himself and to a few of his likes. . . . He preaches 'democracy' and means his own rule. He preaches 'production' and refers to that barren circular movement that simply ensures his existence."

In these and other writings of Hungarian intellectuals, the moral and intellectual collapse of the system—its very essence—had been revealed well before the outbreak of the revolution in October 1956. In a sense, the intellectuals—or some of them, at any rate—had still retained their faith in the viability of certain Marxist ideals: the conviction that society's moral forces would eventually triumph over the party's physical forces and that only a truly socialist-humanist transformation of society could answer the questions left unanswered by totalitarian regimes. In that respect, the movement of the Hungarian intellectuals was the forerunner of the Czech idea of "socialism with a human face" twelve years later.

At the same time, the movement recognized to a greater or lesser extent that the existing anachronisms, distortions, corruptions in the country were organically related to the system; the intellectuals knew now that the "mistakes" that were ascribed to certain party leaders were rooted in Marxist-Leninist theory and were inevitable consequences of "the dictatorship of the proletariat"—a one-party autocracy, and were not merely (as was the official explanation) accidental and atypical results of the "cult of personality." In 1956 Tibor Déry wrote that the Hungarian intellectual movement was faced with a "structural flaw in the system" and added: "We must root out these organic faults that allow our leaders to misuse their power and render us incapable of dealing humanly with one another."

With this essential discovery, the intellectual movement became the leading practical and theoretical force in the country, reasserting, in effect, the traditional role and pattern of intellectuals in Eastern European societies. After decades of silence and servitude, the intellectual emerged again as the embodiment of his nation's conscience. Bonds between the intellectuals and the people were restored and a new national unity forged. No wonder the movement—or rather its participants—were characterized by a sense of joy, freedom, self-confidence that even the rapidly approaching danger could not destroy.

I can clearly recall Hungary in the summer of 1956. Time and again strangers stopped writers on the street to congratulate them on a new poem or article; literature had become, at last, common property. Openly and almost lightheartedly the doctrines and institutions of state were argued about and attacked; the theory of "socialist realism" was as vulnerable as the secret police: neither one of them had been spared. Short-lived yet lively—it seemed, for a moment, the moment of change. Yet it was its very brevity, its shortness, that had important consequences in the weeks to come: the intellectual movement had neither time nor, perhaps, enough energy to work out a program, an alternative, to the party's quickly collapsing political and moral power. The price for the lack of a well-prepared, coherent and positive program was paid on October 23, 1956, when the institutional power collapsed, leaving the country in a political void. It may of course be argued that even the presence of a program would not have saved the Hungarian revolution, what with the swift train of events in the country at large outpacing the demands and actions of those who were trying to lead it. But it is also conceivable that the headlong pace of events and the resulting tragedy could have been averted by a carefully thought-out program of action designed to channel popular passions into a more positive and constructive direction. Whatever the merits of these speculations, it is clear in retrospect that the nature and development of the movement left deep imprints on the national scene. Predominantly emotional, unprogrammatic and, indeed, almost unideological, it gave rise to impassioned articles and essays, mordant and revealing short stories and wonderful poems. Even if it failed to produce any lasting historical or theoretical work contributing to the understanding of that unique and turbulent period of Hungarian history, the movement of the intellectuals created the vision of a humane and moral socialist society and succeeded in setting invaluable historical precedents and guidelines for the continuing struggle of free peoples against totalitarian dictatorships.

Paul Jónás

ECONOMIC ASPECTS*

We have just passed the twentieth anniversary of the Hungarian Revolution and the Polish October, marking the most dramatic period in Europe since the Second World War. Granted the predominant role of political personalities, economic problems were probably the most significant factors in it. The leadership of the countries of East Central Europe had an ideological bias in favor of industrial development at the expense of the agricultural and other sectors. The degree to which industry expanded was thus seen as a measure of the socialist countries' ability to increase their political and military power. Catching up with and surpassing the economically developed countries were frequently proclaimed as the major reasons for demanding more and more sacrifices from the workers in this process of forced industrial development.

After the end of the Second World War the drive toward industrialization continued unabated, and this program meant capital starvation for the agricultural, consumer and tertiary sectors. Large quantities of food supplies were redirected to feed the growing number of industrial workers and to pay for capital imports. As a consequence agricultural investments suffered and the recovery of agricultural production was slowed down. Since wages remained depressed, neither the living standards of the peasants nor those of new industrial workers improved significantly. With the de-Stalinization process, however, some changes were made and the improvement of personal living standards suddenly received a higher priority, which at first meant simply providing more to eat.

In 1956, real per capita disposable income in Hungary was better than, say, in 1952. In spite of this fact, the population was convinced

*With grateful acknowledgment of the financial help of the University of New Mexico's Research Allocation Committee.

that the system was unsound and that wages were intolerably low. One reason for this attitude was a marginal change in the policy of sealing off the country. Some lucky persons were able to visit Vienna; they came back with unbelievable stories of the opulence of the Graben and the Kärntnerstrasse. Western tourists made a lasting impact with their clothing, cameras, watches and other gadgets. The "demonstration effect" worked; dramatically rising expectations made moderate increments in the standard of living unacceptable. At the same time economic issues became the subject of more candid discussion.

In the Petőfi Circle, long debates were held on the state of the economy before large audiences. These were followed by small gatherings at the Kossuth Club and student unions and in apartments, to which those present retreated to exchange more sensitive information over their espresso coffees.

A radical and significant change became apparent among Hungarian intellectuals. Some had never collaborated with the regimes set up by Mátyás Rakosi and the Stalinists. Some had suffered grievously under them. Others, however, had previously not only supported the Stalinist centrally planned course but had also been its official bards, its pampered darlings. Hungarian economists in 1956 were more and more using the same arguments and former Stalinists were often the most vitriolic critics of current economic events. What made them change? Was it blatant opportunism? With some it was. But it would be grotesquely unfair to dismiss all or even the majority as opportunists. In Hungary as in Poland in 1956, many of these intellectuals genuinely rejected the Stalinism they had previously espoused. The Sauls verily became the Pauls and some, indeed, exhibited an almost Pauline enthusiasm and single-mindedness for the new cause. Often, former prison inmates found themselves arguing from the left for a more moderate market-socialist course with former Stalinists who wanted to go further in the process of liberalization. Perhaps only psychologists could attempt to explain some of these conversions; neither the eyewitnesses nor the subjects themselves can do so adequately.

What were the issues discussed at these meetings and gatherings and what was the consensus that can be regarded as the economic root of the Hungarian Revolution? An impressive number of Hungarian intellectuals, many of us alumni of the so-called People's College Movement of 1945-1948, agreed that by 1956 the Hungarian economy with its complexities had outgrown the Stalinist doctrine of industrialization, which had turned into a brake on economic development. We also took a unanimous stand against "giantist" investment policies. Some of our group, who were working in the Central Planning Bureau, complained that they had technical know-how but had to operate in an archaic system that had been-shaped in the Soviet Union in 1931. Complaints were also voiced that factory managers were resisting vital technological improvements because they lacked incentives. A head of a government planning and statistical office complained bitterly that he had to formulate success indicators in obsolete tonnage-oriented targets that failed to reflect actual factor costs or the urgency of demand for commodities.

The consensus was invariably reached that Hungary operated an unbalanced backward economy hobbled by a web of rigid regulations. It also became clear that nobody believed in the golden promise that our children would live in an equitable, just and abundant society and that our sacrifices, waiting lines, unpaid overtime, tensions and compulsory peace bonds were just minor contributions to this goal.

This is not to suggest that the various Hungarian economists bent on reform in 1956 were a totally homogeneous body, but there were common denominators that tended to unify us. In spite of the fact that, in private conversations, almost everybody was critical of the party's stated economic policies (I complained often to my friends in mock dispair: "Can't we finally find a real communist here in this communist country?"), we still never criticized the system vaguely defined as "socialism." We also rejected any so-called return to capitalism. Nor were we in any sense "agents of imperialism," as was later claimed by the satellite regime. True, within our "socialist framework" we resented Soviet domination and exploitation, and in 1956 the fate of Hungarian uranium, which was secretly mined and exported to the Soviet Union, probably worried us too much.

We were looking for a new system of relations among the socialist states, and for this solution we had in mind the agreement between Nikita Khrushchev and Josip Tito. In domestic affairs we totally rejected police coercion and censorship. Most of us also critized the leading role of the party but some argued that with a rejuvenated, democratic, decentralized organization under the leadership of Imre Nagy it was needed to contain conspicuous consumption, a well-known Hungarian characteristic.

It should be stressed constantly that one of the most attractive examples for us was the Yugoslav market-socialist model in which self-managing workers' councils were a major institution. We never failed to quote, with a twinkle, Lenin's slogan: "All power to the Soviets!" We well knew, of course, that *soviets*, i.e., councils of workers, existed neither in the Soviet Union nor in any other Warsaw Pact country.

Our group of economists was invariably joined by other intellectuals, who would report on Western cultural events, such as the plot of Arthur Miller's *Death of a Salesman*, a speech by André Malraux to UNESCO, the current German reaction to the philosophy of György Lukács or new discoveries in the medical sciences.

Our main shortcoming was obviously that we regarded ourselves as the nation's natural élite. Our élitist approach must have offended many nonintellectuals, generating some antiélitist feelings and a certain amount of anti-Semitism.

* * *

Any attempt to analyze in retrospect the so-called economic roots of the Revolution reveals that the economic and in general the political demands of 1956 are still largely those of today in East Central Europe. This is not to suggest that the East Central European situation has not altered since 1956. Only the most hard-core political exiles would deny that politics and the economy have changed for the better. In some countries, such as Hungary, domestic improvements have been enormous.

But the reason why dissatisfaction persists and repeats itself, sometimes with strongly disruptive effects, is that the undoubted material improvements have not been accompanied by the kind of freedom of self-expression that mature societies need and demand. Political institutions, organizations and often practices are still much as they were in Stalin's time.

Our demands were essentially the demands of "revisionist" Czechoslovakia in 1968 and the same burning issues are being discussed today in all the East Central European countries—economic reform and decentralization, the end of police terror and censorship, guarantees of "elementary" freedoms.

János Kádár, whose role after the Hungarian Revolution earned him the loathing of his countrymen, seems to be responsible for things turning out vastly better than anyone dared hope in 1956. In Poland, on the other hand, the gains of October were steadily eroded. By the end of 1957, workers' councils, the main institutional innovation based on the Yugoslav model, had been abolished and freedom of the press had been greatly curtailed. A year later the master plan for economic reform had been permanently shelved. Władysław Gomułka spent the remainder of his fourteen years in power steadily chipping away the pedestal his countrymen had built for him.

The economic roots of the Hungarian Revolution and the Polish October are still unchanged throughout East Central Europe—the desire for better wages and working conditions, for closer consultation, for genuine trade unions, to mention only a few. They also preoccupy the minds of West European or North American workers, but these have means to articulate them not available to their East European counterparts. It was precisely the lack of such means that led to rioting in Poland in 1970 and 1976.

The main reason for this ossified situation lies not in East Central Europe itself nor its often able leaders. The situation has its roots in the deeply conservative, even reactionary, character of the gerontocratic Soviet regime. Until this changes significantly, overambitious investment and production targets will be forced on the population by "unanimously" adopted socioeconomic plans. The underlying message of the plans has remained unchanged: Go for high industrial growth. The Eastern economies will still, however, frequently fail to perform at the programed level deemed appropriate by the planners' unbounded optimism and their eventual recourse will be to "goulash communism." This trend is also encouraged by some Western bankers, who evaluate a relatively low consumption as a plus-factor in assessing nations' creditworthiness. Shortages, sudden, unexpected price increases and the misallocation of resources will turn the attention of East Central European communist intellectuals to the Yugoslav model or some variation of the old dream: socialism without coercion, socialism with a human face. The ideas of Eurocommunism already exercise ideological influence, which is expected to increase, as will demands for equality and independence for each party.

It is not necessary to be a Sovietologist to forecast that Moscow will not tolerate a strong trend toward a polycentric communist bloc. At present stress is on the doctrines of "unification" and "fraternal rapprochement among socialist nations" with the "harmonization of their foreign policies through the political and military organs of the Warsaw Pact." These ideas will be emphasized increasingly and enforced with greater vigilance.

In this sensitive situation how will dissidents, latent or open dissatisfaction, riots, be dealt with? One can expect a stronger reliance on proven methods: repression of human rights, police coercion, forced immigration, mental hospitals, jails, labor camps. East Central Europe will be silenced, seeking only concessions and permissions. The population too well remembers Hungary in 1956 and Czechoslovakia in 1968. The Pan-European Communist Summit Conference in June 1976 formulated the concept of "international voluntary cooperation" to appease the Yugoslav and nonruling European communist parties. It was suggested that this will replace the doctrine of "proletarian internationalism" with all its well-known implications. The party leaders and populations of the East Central European countries, however, will not forget that the Soviet Union is standing by with its well-oiled forces inside their territories or along their borders "to protect the workers against any capitalist restoration." They have learned that no Western nation will actively challenge Soviet military intervention.

East Europe? *Plus ça change* . . . .

POLITICAL ASPECTS

The Hungarian Revolution attracted worldwide attention. People were electrified when young Hungarians demonstrated that the idea of freedom remains a most precious attribute of life, one worth fighting, even dying, for. This was only part of the message of Hungary in 1956, however.

The second part of the message was that this small country, geographically set between antagonistic forces, sought to put together a political concept and structure that would satisfy the opposing ideological and political interests of the Great Powers, and so serve as the basis for Hungary's lasting independence. In retrospect, it seems clear that the first part of the message so overshadowed the second that the latter's great significance was lost on the Western public and governments.

Those in close contact with the events perceived an extraordinary political phenomenon in the revolution. Both the freedom-fighters and the demonstrating masses showed a remarkable sense of political reality and recognized the probable political consequences of their conduct. After October 28, 1956, it was clear to all that Hungary's future hinged on the Soviet decision whether or not to resume military intervention. It was realized that this critical decision depended partly on official reaction in the West, especially in the United States, and partly on the political conduct of the Hungarians. Since no one wanted to give the Soviet Union a pretext to interfere, emotions were toned down and restraint was shown by almost everyone.

Hungarians had every reason to hate the secret police (AVH), who had tortured thousands. It would hardly have been surprising had they taken vengeance by massacring every last one, but it is recorded fact that the opposite was the case. Secret policemen were arrested, taken into custody and told they would face trial when the atmosphere was calm enough for objective judgment. Although such humane behavior was the norm, there were a few exceptional cases where the crowd could not contain its anger. These instances were publicized by Western reporters, who gave the impression that they were usual.

Since the Mátyás Rákosi style of communist rule in Hungary had caused enormous sufferings, it would have been natural if, after its initial victory, the nation had cast out the Communist Party and established an anticommunist state order. Instead, however, a leading political role for a national communist party was desired and demanded by the great noncommunist majority. This seemingly paradoxical behavior of the Hungarians puzzled some Western observers, who looked for a clear-cut anticommunist stand. But this tolerance of the communist party was based on two major considerations.

First, thousands of communists played leading roles in both political and military action during the Revolution, showing that their first loyalty was to country rather than party. A few outstanding examples illustrate this point. The revolutionary climate was created by the Petőfi Circle, a club of liberal, leftist and communist writers, whose daring intellectual protests shook the communist establishment. Imre Nagy, an ardent communist with strong national sentiments, became prime minister by the will of the intellectuals, freedomfighters and noncommunists. The crucial battle against Soviet armored units around the Kilián Barracks in Budapest was led by Pál Maléter, who as a young officer had been indoctrinated by Soviet communists during the Second World War and became a member of the communist party. Numerous party members with middle-ranking positions fought and died for the country in the Revolution.

Secondly, it was generally seen that friendly cooperation between the large noncommunist majority and those communists who honestly sought a happier future for Hungary was essential to pacify the Soviet leadership. It was plain that Hungary had to demonstrate by political acts that it did not want a conflict with the Soviet Union nor intend to alter its foreign policy radically, but rather desired a peaceful settlement with the Soviet Union in whose menacing shadow it had to live.

In short, the Hungarian people realized that they had voluntarily to pay the political price of the lasting benefits they sought. What that price was seemed obvious. A mixed political system had to be created in which the Stalinists (who might be called antinoncommunists) and the ultrarightwing anticommunists would be offset by the cooperation of a number of noncommunist democratic parties and one national communist party. This was clearly reflected in the reorganization of the Nagy government on October 31 as a coalition in which the almost exclusively communist government was joined by representatives of the Smallholders', the Social Democratic and the National Peasant (Petőfi) Parties.

Participation in a coalition government under communist leadership was an unpalatable and frightening idea for numerous Smallholders and Social Democrats, who had suffered imprisonment and torture during the Rákosi terror years. Several Smallholder leaders believed that, since the party had gained an absolute majority in the 1945 elections, it had a right to a majority role now. In addition, the Smallholders had an enormously popular and respected leader who had spent ten years in a Soviet prison camp, Béla Kovács, their former secretary general, who had vocally opposed the Soviet domination of Hungary in the postwar years. The truth is that while Imre Nagy was the trusted leader of one million disillusioned communist party members, Kovács was the idol of the great noncommunist masses. As a trusted friend of Kovács, I was working with him continuously during this time. We discussed participation in the Nagy government for hours on end. Our final agreement to it was based on our judgment that only a left-of-center government and strict neutrality could preempt a return Soviet military invasion and simultaneously secure Western political help. Kovács himself did not expect any help from the West but he halfheartedly accepted my argument that Western self-interest dictated political help to Hungary.

The Social Democrats, whose real leaders, headed by Anna Kéthly, had been arrested *en masse* by Rákosi in the late 1940s, were also engaged in emotional discussions in those days of October 1956 about their possible participation in the Nagy government. A decision to join another coalition with the communists was extremely difficult for them. Much the same debate was going on in the National Peasant Party, too.

Eventually, sober consideration of the future led both the Smallholders and the Social Democrats to enter the coalition in order to try to save the country's independence.

The recent neutralization of Austria and Finland's balancing between East and West by taking a somewhat Soviet-slanted position of neutrality were not lost on Hungary. It appeared logical to believe that, since the policies of those two countries were acceptable to the Soviet Union, Hungary could adapt their examples into a political concept that would be tolerated by the Soviet Union and at the same time would elicit Western support.

A Titoist solution was unacceptable to the mass of the population and was considered by the politicians as likely to be the most objectionable position to the Soviet Union. It was never seriously considered by the noncommunist parties. The general mood of the nation, as expressed in written demands and in words, strongly favored national reconciliation through a left-of-center political structure and working out a *modus vivendi* with the Soviet Union.

The record is clear. National unity was reestablished through mutual compromise designed to prevent the political pendulum from swinging too far to either left or right. In all frankness, we who were eyewitnesses of those events, who took an active part in them and who were steadfast in our democratic, noncommunist beliefs had to recognize that the interests of our country demanded our participation in a political settlement which of necessity veered more to the left than we would have liked. This left-of-center arrangement was particularly clearly reflected in all the statements about the future socioeconomic structure of the country. Neither the freedom-fighters nor any of the reorganized traditional democratic parties were ready to uproot the existing nationalized economic structure in order to replace it with an admittedly much more desirable private-enterprise system. Common sense warned us that such a change would occasion a Soviet cry of "counterrevolution" and would probably be misunderstood in the West, where liberal and radical intellectuals might think that Hungary wished to restore a rightist-conservative semifeudal political system. The truth is also that the nationalization of large industries and estates had been accepted by the majority of the population as the natural cure for the ills of the past. Hundreds of thousands approved the slogan: "We won't give back the land or factories."

The public gave a clear mandate to the Hungarian revolutionary government to take decisive political action. New Soviet military movements in the provinces allowed no time for hesitation. Counteracting this military danger by political means was the only feasible course. So on November 1, 1956, the revolutionary government declared Hungary's neutrality and withdrawal from the Warsaw Pact. At the same time the government announced that Hungary was ready to renegotiate its future relations with the Soviet Union in an atmosphere of national independence and respect for each other's interests.

The declaration of neutrality was dispatched to all foreign diplomatic missions in Budapest and was sent by special telex to the secretary general of the United Nations, Dag Hammarskjöld. The cable, which included a request to the four Great Powers to protect Hungary's neutrality, was received at the United Nations in New York on November 1, 1956, at 12:27 p.m.

It was a historic moment. The Western Powers were given an un-expected opportunity to bring about favorable changes in East Central Europe by taking a strong stand against the Soviet Union in the United Nations. Specifically, it was realistically expected that the Western Powers would demand an urgent special session to discuss the Hungarian question. But unfortunately, Western, particularly American, attention was focused at the time on the Suez crisis. While the Hungarian cable was crawling slowly through the United Nations, the Soviet Union announced that negotiations had started between the Soviet and Hungarian governments, so that there was no need for United Nations discussion of the Hungarian question. Western, parti-cularly American, diplomats accepted the Soviet announcement at face value, so that the Western Powers, under United States leader-ship, acted with considerable delay. They requested an emergency session of the General Assembly only on November 3 and were satis-fied when it was scheduled for Monday, November 5.

The clock of history, however, was racing. In the early hours of Sunday, November 4, twenty-four hours before the General Assem-bly session, the Soviet Union invaded Hungary with the full-scale machinery of war.

Hungarian views about the real value of the opportunity offered by the Hungarian Revolution for bringing about a desirable settle-ment in East Central Europe may be doubted by others, but a sharp observer of the European scene, Hugh Seton-Watson, has written: "It is always more dangerous to upset a status quo than to maintain one: between 28 October and 3 November the status quo was favor-able to the West, not to the Soviet Union. The task of Western diplo-macy should have been to alarm the Soviet government while offer-ing inducements, in the form of a wider settlement in Europe, for negotiation, meanwhile insisting that the legal government of Hun-gary must be left undisturbed. It is, of course, true that the Western Powers did not wish a world war for the sake of Hungary, but the Soviet government was also afraid of world war. The element of un-certainty could have been made to work in favor of the West as long as Nagy maintained himself."[1]

The West did not recognize its opportunity. When the United States denounced its European allies for the Suez action, the Soviet

Union realized that it had a free hand in Hungary. The most discouraging aspect of Western inaction over Hungary is that there existed no contingency plans in the West for such an eventuality. This is particularly regrettable since numerous events in 1955 and early 1956 in the Soviet sphere pointed to major changes in Soviet policies. They included Nikita Khrushchev's Canossa pilgrimage to Tito in May 1955; the signing of the Austrian State Treaty by the Soviet Union in May 1955, leading to the withdrawal of Soviet troops and the neutralization of Austria; the Soviet Union's startling statement in September 1955 that it would recede Porkkala to the Finns;[2] and Khrushchev's famous speech in February 1956 denouncing Stalin and Stalinism.

Khrushchev gave numerous signals in 1955 that indicated that the new Soviet leadership would be open to a rapprochement with the Western Powers. In this new international political climate Khrushchev showed moderation even in a situation as critical as the Poznań uprising in June 1956. There were ample grounds to believe in the first week of the Hungarian Revolution that the time was ripe for a major Western political initiative to try to achieve the concepts drafted by the US State Department in 1944. Their substance was described by Arthur Schlesinger, Jr., in the following terms:"Governments in Eastern Europe could be sufficiently to the left to allay Soviet suspicion, but sufficiently representative of the center and petit-bourgeois elements. . . . A string of New Deal states, of Finlands . . . seemed a reasonable compromise."[3]

In all probability, the second Soviet intervention in Hungary could have been prevented by the Western Powers if during those critical days they had offered the Soviet Union high-level negotiations on a détente in their mutual relations and a new European settlement. In retrospect, it is reasonable to believe that European East-West negotiations at that time could have saved Hungary and yielded much more favorable results to the West than those reached at Helsinki in 1975. In this context, a comparison may be attempted between a hypothetical détente in 1956 and the actual Helsinki détente in 1975.

In 1956, Khrushchev probably would have considered Western scientific and technological help worth political concessions. In the seventies, the Soviet Union received this without any *quid pro quo*. In 1956, the reestablishment of a multiparty coalition government in one country, combined with a Finnish type of friendship treaty, could have been accepted by the Soviet Union as a realistic trade-off for Western scientific help and commercial ties. The neutralization of Hungary under the supervision and guarantee of the four Great

Powers could have been included in a scheme for a new settlement, simply because the Warsaw Pact existed at that time only on paper and Hungary's strategic importance had been decreased by the neutralization of Austria.

Helsinki marks a significant political shift in the European area. While in the forties and fifties, East Central Europe was the focal point of East-West contest, in recent years the future of Western Europe has emerged as the most critical issue. The major deficiency of the Helsinki agreements is that they have indirectly strengthened the legal basis of communist party activities in Western Europe while offering no reciprocal inducement for the reappearance of democratic parties in East Central Europe.

It is fashionable to concentrate only on one unexpected and favorable side effect of the Helsinki agreements. The "third basket" of them has supplied some legal basis for the expression of intellectual dissent within the Soviet sphere. We should not belittle this, but nor should we neglect the side effects unfavorable to the West. The latter include above all the strengthening and growth of public acceptance of the communist parties in Western Europe. Whatever expectations Eurocommunism arouses on the humanistic plane, it must be recognized that on the political plane it would give an impetus to the Finlandization of Western Europe, which may also be propelled by other factors, including the mesmerizing effect of ever growing Soviet military might, domestic socioeconomic difficulties in certain states and discord among the Western European countries. The Soviet naval buildup in both the Mediterranean and North Seas in the last decade, the present situation in Turkey and Greece, Britain's economic difficulties and the increased activities of the communist parties in Italy, France and elsewhere in Western Europe are the new reality.

The general trends in the East Central European countries also deserve attention. In the last decade most of the communist governments have successfully convinced their populations that improvement of the material quality of life is the only realistic goal open to them. Several countries have had considerable success in this respect. This new materialistic atmosphere and the self-evident dependence on the political will of Moscow have stifled the pursuit of bolder political aspirations. But Eurocommunism may induce a desire for greater independence and the freer expression of political thought. While no one will dare to talk about neutrality, such a desire may grow unnoticed in the minds of those dissatisfied with the restrictiveness of one-party communist rule.

In summary, in 1956 an opportunity was given the West to seek, or at least attempt to seek, a favorable political solution for East Central Europe. The opportunity was missed. In contrast, nineteen years later, in Helsinki, a détente was formalized that may automatically stimulate the Finlandization of Western Europe. It is my fervent hope that the danger will soon be recognized by the West and will be followed by studies of a series of potential alternative counterinitiatives. In such a process, the concept of the Hungarian Revolution could supply inspiration.

NOTES

1. G. Hugh N. Seton-Watson, *Neither War Nor Peace* (New York, 1960), p. 343.

2. The Porkkala military base was located less than twenty miles from Helsinki. The Soviet right to use it was assured by the Finnish-Soviet peace treaty of 1947.

3. Arthur Schlesinger, Jr., "Origins of the Cold War," *Foreign Affairs*, October, 1967, p. 37.

George G. Heltai

INTERNATIONAL ASPECTS

Analyzing the internal and external aspirations of the Hungarian Revolution leads to the conclusion that in many ways it belongs more to the nineteenth than to the twentieth century. It was directed at aims (moral resurrection, freedom, independence) that the past century should have fulfilled. It was an outburst of moral indignation, the culmination of an evolutionary process that started in the whole Soviet empire after Stalin's death and received a forceful impetus in Nikita Khrushchev's revelations at the twentieth congress of his party. Although the underlying causes—betrayal of ideas, legal murder and imprisonment of millions, mental and physical colonization of ten millions—have been the same in all East Central European countries, there was a certain inequality in the process. This happened not simply as a result of national particularities but as a consequence of the isolation imposed by the Stalinist system and by the different degrees of destruction of the political and intellectual life executed by the local proconsuls of the central power. By reducing to nothing all social bodies, the regime imprisoned every inhabitant of its empire in permanent fear. At the first opportunity a desire developed to deliver the oppressed from this fear and from the lies and loneliness springing from alienation. It was a catharsis, a moral drive testifying that the dead bodies of innocent victims still weighed heavily on men's minds and prepared them for sacrifices. It was a movement for ethical corrections, silent and clandestine in some countries, open and noisy in others, but mostly an internal affair—with some external ramifications—in all the countries.

In Hungary it became a movement for reforms, faceless and hopeless until it found the embodiment of its hopes and aspirations in Imre Nagy, the former prime minister, whose personality and program attracted the confidence of the nation. Deposed by the rulers of the regime, he became the symbol of lost expectations and the hope of renewal. Imre Nagy emphasized the causal relationship between internal and external policies and the movement hitherto preoccupied with the former now became involved in the latter, too. The Yugoslav developments and especially the Polish events of 1956 had been watched intently by the Hungarians. The changes in Poland, the apparent success of the Polish reform movement and the reinstatement of its leader to power had served as an example. Yet nobody was dreaming of, or preparing for, a revolution.

Nevertheless it happened. The arrogance of the government and the provocation of Soviet arms turned a demonstration held in sympathy with the Poles into an insurrection. From the small hours of the morning of October 24 a spontaneous revolution of the youth ran its own course for the restitution of human dignity. It had no leaders, only participants; no plans, only actions. It created its own revolutionary organs—the workers' councils—and formulated its own foreign policy expressed in one sentence: "Russki, go home."

Although Imre Nagy was appointed prime minister (chairman of the Council of Ministers) by the communist party leadership, for almost four days he was kept as a virtual prisoner in the party headquarters. There he was informed of the developments in the country in the form of alarmist tales fabricated in the party center. The days called for action, but he had no means to act. During three days of total isolation, events had passed far beyond his conceptions. Revolution had now extended itself over the entire country, the government had collapsed, the party which he wanted to save and purify was in shambles. It was only after the intervention of high-ranking Soviet emissaries (Anastas Mikoyan and Mikhail Suslov) that he regained his freedom of action. On October 27 he took the first steps to assess the internal and international situation. He received hundreds of delegates and sent out his deputies to the still fighting groups to restore order, his aim being the immediate halting of bloodshed. In the afternoon he consulted his advisers on matters of foreign policy.* The information gathered was scattered and not completely reliable. The foreign ministry had ceased to function and, even if it had not, the value of its reports would have been doubtful. There was a consensus: nothing could be done in matters of foreign policy without provoking the Soviets. Consequently, it was agreed that the first task of the new government should be the removal of

---

* Geza Losonczy and the writer.

the irritating presence of alien troops and investigation of the pre-text under which they were sent in. At this juncture the prime min-ister revealed the essence of his negotiations with Mikoyan and Suslov. If order was to be restored, the Soviet government would be willing to reevaluate the situation, recognize the Hungarian changes and withdraw its troops.

Twenty-four hours later, on the afternoon of the 28th, Radio Budapest announced a cease-fire, and the Nagy government recog-nized as its own the demands of the insurgents. At 5:00 p.m. Nagy himself stood before the microphone and unambiguously took his stand by the Revolution, indeed at its head. He inspired his listeners as he said that the new government had been born from the battles of the Revolution, that it was the government of national unity, of independence and of democratic socialism and would be the genu-ine expresser of the popular will. He reported to the nation that the Hungarian government had come to an agreement with the Soviet government, that the Soviet forces would commence their with-drawal from the capital immediately and that the two governments would institute discussions to regulate Hungarian-Soviet relations on the basis of the equality and national independence of socialist states. The following days it seemed as if the unthinkable had come to pass. The fighting stopped, the withdrawal of Russian troops—even though slow—did begin. Budapest came back to life.

It appeared that the Revolution might now implement the long-coveted reforms. The Soviet-Hungarian relationship, however, still remained a thorny problem, and one to be approached with the greatest prudence. To preclude the return of the Soviet troops, should not the government investigate the possibilities of a declara-tion of neutrality and the release of Hungary from the Warsaw Pact?* Nagy advocated restraint. His primary concern was to avoid any step that might be regarded as provocative and that could offer a pretext for the Russians to suppress the revolution. The Soviet troops were still stationed on Hungary's territory and even their withdrawal from Budapest was proceeding with alarming slowness. No steps, no inquiries should be made that could arouse Soviet suspicion. Precisely for this reason the prime minister planned to put aside momentarily all other problems to concentrate on the task of

---

* In one of his Memoranda to the Central Committee of the Hungarian Workers' Party (communist party) and delivered personally to the Soviet embassy in July 1956, Nagy had already dealt with the idea "to examine the possibility of neutralizing Hungary on the Austrian pattern".

political reorganization and the stabilization of national unity, so that the government might offer to the Soviet leaders a satisfactory guarantee to accomplish the complete withdrawal of their forces.

The West reacted sympathetically to the Hungarian events. Public opinion supported the Revolution and the Nagy government, in spite of the emphasis Western correspondents laid on its progressive features. Only Radio Free Europe attacked Nagy and incited its audience to continuation of the fight. Western governmental reactions were unknown. Members of the Hungarian foreign service had no way to approach responsible politicians; the overwhelming majority did not even speak the language of the countries to which they were accredited; some put themselves under Russian command (like the one who on October 27 protested against any possible interference on the part of the UN Security Council in the affairs of his country). The representatives of Great Britain, France and the United States in Budapest made no contacts with the government in the first days (the US embassy hoisted a white flag during the days of fighting) and later, when asked, assured the government of their personal sympathies but had no information about the intention of their respective cabinets.

From the countries of the Soviet bloc the reports varied. There was enormous popular support, but vicious governmental attacks in Rumania and Czechoslovakia, and almost total backing from Poland and Yugoslavia. The Polish and Yugoslav ambassadors transmitted personal messages from Władysław Gomułka and Josip Tito, reiterating their solidarity with Nagy and their sympathies for the success of the revolution. Gomułka even offered his government's services to mediate between Hungary and the USSR if necessary.

Internally the consolidation progressed: the one-party system was abolished, representatives of the democratic parties took their seats in the new government, and the heartbeat of the country began to slow down to normal. There were hopes, but the retreat of the Russian troops was taking an agonizingly long time. On the afternoon of the 30th Mikoyan and Suslov arrived back in Budapest. In their talks with Nagy they appeared sympathetic to the latest political developments in Hungary. They agreed to open the forthcoming Hungarian-Soviet negotiations with discussion of methods of evacuating all Soviet troops from Hungary. Not only would military units be withdrawn from Budapest, the Soviet representatives said, but some detachments would immediately be transferred out of the country. The pledge seemed confirmed when Soviet military units evacuated

Budapest on the evening of October 30 and turned protection of public buildings over to the newly formed Hungarian National Guard. Finally they informed Nagy of the draft of a Soviet government statement scheduled to appear in *Pravda* the following day. The statement asserted that the Soviet Union wished to review its relations with neighboring states, that it basically accepted the legality of Hungarian demands and would withdraw its troops from Budapest.

On October 31 the statement was published in *Pravda*. In terms of Hungarian hopes, the published version was even more satisfactory than the draft had been and in parts even seemed to echo Nagy's own words:

> The countries of the great commonwealth of socialist nations can build their mutual relations only on the principles of complete equality, respect for territorial integrity, national independence and sovereignty, and noninterference in one another's internal affairs. . . . There have been many difficulties, unresolved problems and downright mistakes, including mistakes in the mutual relations of the socialist countries—violations and errors which demeaned the principle of equality in relations among the socialist states. [Several clichés on the role of Soviet troops in Budapest followed.] The Soviet government is prepared to enter into appropriate negotiations with the government of the Hungarian People's Republic and other members of the Warsaw treaty on the question of the presence of Soviet troops on the territory of Hungary.

With the publication of the Soviet declaration the revolution reached a delirious stage—the streets of Budapest were full of joyous masses of people smelling victory.

At the same time ominous news reached the government. From the dawn on, reports and telephone calls poured in, warning that new Soviet troops were crossing the border into Hungary at Záhony. The General Staff confirmed the reports, stating: "At present the invasion is not full-scale, but it is possible that these troops are merely advance units of a considerable military force."

The report dashed the hopes that had blossomed since the previous night. And shortly thereafter came the second blow, cables confirming the serious attacks of British, French and Israeli forces on Egypt. Nagy hastily conferred with his colleagues. First Suez: horrible timing using the Hungarian Revolution and the Soviet preoccupation with it for this aggression. After longer analysis a ray of hope broke through. The United States was not participating in this adventure, was deeply interested in laying hands on the Anglo-French heritage in the Middle East and Africa and would try to avoid destruction of the region as far as possible. Probably, then, it would intervene, mediate and eventually force its allies to withdraw their troops, thus appeasing the angered Soviet government, which too felt committed to the Middle East and North Africa. As a minimal recompense the US could demand Soviet nonintervention in Hungary. Then, the conference turned to the "more serious" problem of the possible invasion of Hungary. Since there was no Hungarian army or air force to speak of, and hardly any available ammunition, the arrival of new Soviet troops meant the end of the Revolution if they were the harbingers of an all-out Soviet action. There was also the equally dangerous possibility that the flammable revolutionary forces would be provoked by the troop movements into mounting a suicidal rifle attack on Soviet tanks. To prevent such a disaster the conference decided to keep the morning report secret. Everyone at the conference agreed that it was imperative to obtain Soviet guarantees that the infiltration of troops would not continue and for Hungary to leave the Warsaw Pact. The fact that Soviet military units entered the country without the knowledge or approval of the Hungarian government was a clear violation of the Warsaw Protocol and ample justification in itself for such a step. Later the government discussed various alternatives, agreeing on the necessity of reassuring the Soviet Union about the Hungarian government's future plans. Mikoyan should not only be informed that Hungary intended to pursue a course of neutrality, he should also be convinced that a Hungary belonging to no power group and friendly to the USSR—that is, a neutral, socialist Hungary—could be extremely valuable in solving international problems and in helping the Soviet Union to establish a *modus vivendi* with the West. No other action was decided. The general feeling was that, because of the peculiar character of the Revolution, a good deal of mistrust and misconceptions both in the West and in the USSR would have to be overcome before negotiations of this kind could begin, and that it would be premature and dangerous to ask now for Great Power recognition of Hungary's neutrality. The Russians would regard any talks between Hungary and the West as a "provocation" and might use it as a pretext for invading Hungary. Secret talks were also out of the question because in the prevailing atmosphere nothing could be kept secret.

Talks with Mikoyan and Suslov dragged on into the afternoon. At a cabinet meeting after the talks, Nagy reported that the situation did not look hopeless; the Soviet representatives had stressed that the new troop arrivals were routine in character. Minimal forces had been dispatched to assure the orderly withdrawal of Soviet troops, and Mikoyan and Suslov had expressed a disposition to begin talks on revising the Warsaw Treaty. They made no commitment on Hungarian neutrality, implying that Hungary would in one form or another remain a member of the remodeled pact. They expressed confidence in the new coalition government. Should further changes that would not affect the socialist character of the government be necessary to sustain the coalition, they could consider them.

News of the negotiations spread through Budapest like wildfire, while reports of the departing Soviet units and information asserting that the new troops had not left the northern border area seemed to confirm that things were going well. The General Staff took a favorable view of the developments, and by night-time the atmosphere in the capital was peaceful. Nagy and his associates worked on the new government platform.

The quiet ended abruptly. Early next morning (November 1) a courier from the ministry of defense delivered a message for the prime minister: more Soviet units with about 300 tanks had crossed the Hungarian border and were moving toward the center of the country. Within minutes the cabinet was convened. Nagy, looking calm and determined, sent a protesting cable to Marshal Kliment Voroshilov, the Soviet head of state, and called for the Soviet ambassador, who arrived at 9:00 a.m. Ambassador Yuri Andropov claimed he knew nothing but would get in touch with his government without delay.

Young workers from the outskirts of Budapest burst into the crammed waiting rooms of the prime minister with alarming news: the Soviets had not left, they had dug in around the workers' housing projects in the outer suburbs. New reports from the General Staff revealed that Soviet armored divisions—more than 1,000 tanks—were massed in the northwest, aiming at the capital.

Andropov finally returned. Suave and amiable, he explained that no military units had crossed into Hungary. The troops were actually NKVD (secret police) units required because discipline had apparently disintegrated among some of the Soviet forces and because it was imperative to forestall disorder during withdrawal. Unconvinced, Nagy demanded that the Soviet government reply to his complaints within an hour.

At noon Ambassador Andropov telephoned Moscow's reply: the Soviet government upheld its declaration of October 30 with regard to the withdrawal of Soviet forces from Hungary and maintained its willingness to discuss the modification of the Warsaw Pact. To this end, it requested the Hungarian government to appoint a political commission to deal with questions of principle and a military commission for the technical aspects.

Nagy asked for a definite pledge that troop movements would halt immediately. Andropov's answer was in the negative.

For the Hungarians around Imre Nagy, the Soviet intention was evident: the suppression of the Revolution. In no sense could 1,000 tanks be regarded as a police force—not even in the USSR—and as these tanks inevitably met with popular resistance, the Russians would have an excellent excuse for overrunning the country. To prevent this and disarm the resistance was almost impossible—and who would be willing to commit such treason? Furthermore, the outcome of such an effort would probably be a civil war, with Moscow gleefully watching the nation slaughter itself. The only solution seemed to be for Hungary to announce immediately its withdrawal from the Warsaw Pact and to declare its neutrality.

The Council of Ministers, having established that the Soviet Union, by the dispatch of fresh divisions, had *de facto* invalidated the Warsaw Treaty, determined on Hungary's withdrawal and, at the same time, the proclamation of its neutrality.

The cabinet also discussed the text of notes to be sent to the UN and to the heads of accredited diplomatic missions in Budapest.

In the late afternoon Andropov was invited to the session of the cabinet. Here Imre Nagy disclosed the latest detailed evidence of Soviet troop advances, explained the causes for the Hungarian government's withdrawal from the Warsaw Treaty and read the declaration of neutrality, emphasizing that Hungary had no desire to join any power bloc.

As the Soviet troop movements continued, the Hungarian government sent a telegram to the secretary general of the UN with the text of the declaration of neutrality and with a request that the four Great Powers guarantee Hungarian neutrality. The Hungarian government also requested that the Hungarian question be placed on the agenda of the next UN General Assembly meeting.

A strange relief, an *alea jacta est* atmosphere, prevailed now over Hungary, in the government. The nation was in the hands of the Great Powers; were they good hands? The international reaction was generally favorable. Poland and Yugoslavia expressed their support through their ambassadors. China was noncommittal. Rumania threatened sanctions, and the diplomatic representatives of the Western countries expressed joyous surprise and promised to inform their governments about the urgent needs of Hungary.

Reports of further Soviet troop movements on November 2 aroused little alarm because of optimism over the moves at the UN.

While waiting for an answer from the United Nations—after 12 hours still nothing—the government sought to gain time. New notes, new protests were sent to the Soviet government, which in its answers requested a list of names of delegates to the previously proposed negotiations. The Hungarians could choose the site of political negotiations; the Soviets proposed that the military negotiations be held in Budapest.

The atmosphere became one of feverish activity, although concentration was almost impossible. Hungary was waiting for Dag Hammarskjöld's reply. Then a teletype message from the UN arrived. The secretary general wanted proof that Nagy had really signed the authorization of a Hungarian legation secretary delegated to the assembly. . . .

That afternoon Nagy met with his closest advisers. About 24 hours had passed since the note had been sent and it was now evident that the UN had failed to place the Hungarian issue on the General Assembly agenda. A new cable was sent requesting Security Council intervention. The waiting continued . . . .

November 3 was a beautiful, sunny autumn day. The cabinet seemed enveloped by a feeling of peace and confidence. The Hungarian military delegation was negotiating with the Soviet generals. The reports were encouraging; speedy withdrawal of Soviet troops had been agreed upon, only technicalities remained to be discussed. After an adjournment, the talks were to be resumed that evening at Soviet headquarters in Tököl, just outside the capital. Until midnight the Hungarian delegation sent regular reports from Soviet headquarters. Ten minutes after midnight radio communication was interrupted. Soviet secret police had seized the Hungarian delegation.

At dawn on November 4, the people of Budapest were awakened by the sound of cannon. At 5:30 a.m. Radio Kossuth went on the air: "This is Imre Nagy, chairman of the Council of Ministers of the Hungarian People's Republic. At dawn this morning Soviet forces attacked our capital city. . . . Our troops are in action."

Béla K. Kirdly

MILITARY ASPECTS

What happened in Hungary in October and November 1956 has been
called by a variety of names: "revolt," "uprising"—or "counterrevolution" by its opponents. In the socialist states of Eastern Europe it
has been reduced to a nonevent and, if reference to it is unavoidable,
it is passed off as "the events of 1956." It was, however, a revolution, pure and simple. Popular will swept away a regime that had
been imposed by the Soviet Union, modeled after it and maintained
in power by its forces. Violence was not the purpose of the revolutionaries but, when forced to, they met violence with violence. One
of the most remarkable features of the Revoluton—and what made it
a revolution in the real sense of the word—was the rapid establishment of new institutions from the lowest level to the central state
administration. In villages, towns and counties, in civilian and military organizations, in schools, factories, collective farms and the
courts popular gatherings, often by acclamation, set up new govern-
ing bodies called "revolutionary councils" or "national committees."
Whatever their names, they all had certain characteristics in common:
they responded to the will of the majority; those elected to positions
of responsibility enjoyed the trust of the majority; communists were
not discriminated against—in fact, party members and even some officials gained election in a number of places. In short, democracy
was at work at the grass roots, evidence of how attractive this form
of government is even in a country where totalitarian theory, education and practice had been enforced for a decade.

The prevailing view is that the Hungarian Revolution of 1956 was
a fiasco. So widespread is this opinion that it seems almost futile to
challenge it. Yet issue must be taken: the Revolution was a victory.
What, after all, is a revolution if not the overthrow of an old order
and the installation of a new political and/or social and/or economic

system? A revolution is a domestic event and domestically Hungary's October was completely successful. There existed no domestic forces that could have toppled the new regime and restored the old or set up anything against the general will of the revolutionaries. Imre Nagy's last government, a coalition of the traditional democratic parties, accorded with the Hungarian people's wishes and reflected their persuasions. It reintroduced the basic features of political democracy but did not touch the main framework of public ownership of the means of production—that is, it left the socialist structure of Hungary's economy unchanged. The Nagy government intended to hold free general elections and it is moot whether a future Parliament would have left things as they were on November 4, 1956, and whether the Hungarian people would have wished to go on living in a socialist economic system. My personal opinion is that they would. What is beyond question, however, is that there was an overwhelming desire for a democratic government established through free democratic processes. Had Hungary been left alone, the future of democracy in this small nation may be taken for granted. In this key sense the Revolution was undoubtedly a triumph.

What suppressed the Hungarian democratic socialist government was not a domestic force but a foreign one: the Soviet army. The facts are too well known to require any documentary evidence. The question that can be raised is whether the Soviet military intervention in Hungary amounted to an international war.[1]

International war is the massive application of armed might between states, prosecuted systematically in order to destroy an opponent's will or means to fight. The purpose of war is the achievement of certain objectives, such as the cession of territory, the imposition of a religion or ideology, or the securing of economic advantage. When the Soviet forces invaded Budapest at dawn on October 24, 1956, and began indiscriminate destruction, they were interfering directly in Hungary's internal affairs. It is now known that Ernő Gerő, the first secretary of the Hungarian Socialist Workers' Party, not only consented to the intervention but may even have entreated immediate Soviet armed protection, which the Soviet leaders may at first have hesitated to afford. Yet a Soviet armed incursion did not necessarily add up to an act of war. As in Berlin in 1953 and Czechoslovakia in 1968, the intention and hope could have been to intimidate the Hungarians by the show of force into reestablishing the Soviet type of socialism and a regime loyal to Moscow. However, when the Soviet invasion was set in motion again on November 1,

when the airports were gradually occupied and massive armed columns advanced on Budapest, when an iron ring of armor had been
closed around the capital by November 3, and when Soviet artillery
on the night of November 3-4 opened fire first on Kiskunhalas and
then on barracks all over the country, it became obvious that the
Soviet socialist Great Power had premeditatedly launched a full-scale
armed offensive against democratic socialist Hungary. This military
operation was executed systematically in order to smash Hungary's
armed forces and to shatter the nation's will to resist. The Soviet
government evidently intended to reimpose its own brand of socialism through a regime that it was going to install in Hungary—and
this is precisely what it did. Soviet political and military actions cor-
responded exactly to the elements of war. I have no shadow of
doubt that after November 1 the Union of Soviet Socialist Republics
was at war with the democratic socialist state of Hungary. November
1 is the date the invasion and indeed the war began; only actual
shooting did not erupt till November 4. The Soviet Union has the
dubious distinction of being the first socialist state in history to
make war on another socialist state.

* * *

The attitude of the armed forces is generally decisive in a revolution. If they stand by the old regime, the forces of change have
slender, if any, chance of gaining the upper hand. If the army stays
neutral, the revolutionaries have some chance of success. If the army
turns against the old regime, the revolution will almost certainly triumph. When the first shots of the revolution rang out on the evening
of October 23, 1956, outside the Radio Building in Budapest, troops
already on the alert were rushed in to break up the demonstrators.
The party leaders hardly doubted that the army would sweep the
square clear. The rank and file had been inculcated with party doctrine all their young adult lives. They had been barely into their
teens when the communists took power and had never known any
but a totalitarian government. They bore Soviet arms, equipment
and uniforms; they were under the constant surveillance of the
secret police (AVH), who were to be found right down to company
level; they were officered by cadres trained in the Soviet Union or in
military schools in Hungary patterned after Soviet models; their regi-
mental commanders upwards had at their elbows Soviet advisers who
were the real directors of operations. Under such circumstances, how
could the army act other than in accordance with the dictates of the
party?

But soldiers anywhere with a universal draft are nothing but young people in uniform. So it was that the troops rushed to the Radio Building on October 23 had sentiments little different from those of the youngsters in civilian clothes lining the streets and chanting revolutionary slogans into their ears. The marching columns were being in effect counterindoctrinated by their peers, if it was even necessary. At the very first confrontation between military and civilian, the young men under arms refused to fire on their compatriots. At that selfsame moment the future of the old regime was called into serious doubt by the army itself. The Hungarian "People's Army" proved that its prime loyalty was to the people rather than to the party.

The genesis of the People's Army had been long drawn out. The "socialization" of the government, society and economy had been completed much sooner. At the end of the Second World War the Hungarian Army had been all but disbanded. Since the Soviet Army had remained in Hungary, there was no need for the Hungarian Army, which in any case might have posed a threat to the establishment of the totalitarian regime. So, as in other countries in the area under Soviet control, the Hungarian army was reduced to its bare bones.[2] Its socialization was begun at last in September 1948 and was pushed forward much more rapidly than had been that of the civilian branches of the government. The process was complete by the time Lieutenant General György Pálffy, the inspector general of the army, was executed in September 1949.

The socialization of the army and its simultaneous and equally speedy reorganization, rearmament and expansion were prompted by the Yugoslav-Soviet crisis. The Soviet Union's military and technical advisers left Belgrade on March 18, 1948, and on June 28 Yugoslavia was expelled from the Cominform. Hungary, already the Soviet Union's obedient ally under the rule of Mátyás Rákosi, was now in the forefront of the ideological, political and military confrontation with Yugoslavia. The hitherto neglected armed forces thus suddenly became a key factor for the party and government. What happened to them between September 1948 and the summer of 1949 was similar to the socialization of the civilian government but with other elements made necessary by the specific nature of the military. Military socialization included replacing the supreme command with party leaders (Politburo member Mihály Farkas became minister of defense and Central Committee member Sándor Nogrády, his first deputy); reorganizing political control on the Soviet pattern, including introduction of the *politruk* system by which political officers became cocommanders of the troops; gradually substituting party functionaries for the professional officers of middle and junior rank; training party cadres in the Soviet Union or Hungary for professional military command; introducing Soviet military doctrine and regulations; engaging in mass anti-Yugoslav propaganda; rearming with Soviet weaponry and equipment; retooling Hungarian industry to manufacture Soviet types of arms and weapons, and integrating Hungary into Soviet war plans. The whole process was executed under the watchful gaze of an ever increasing number of Soviet advisers.

Even while the army was still being refashioned, its integration into Soviet plans for an anti-Yugoslav war was begun. The first such strategic plans were completed before the Rajk trials of 1949, and were revised annually to adjust them to the army's increase in strength. The Hungarian Army's role in these Soviet strategic plans was straightforward: it was to be the first wave of a Soviet offensive against Yugoslavia. The Hungarian Army was to attack between the Danube and Tisza rivers, break through the Yugoslav frontier defenses, advance to Novi Sad, cross the Danube and occupy the Fruška Gora hills to establish a bridgehead south of the Danube, from which Soviet forces could overrun Belgrade itself. Rumanian, Bulgarian and Albanian forces were assigned similar missions in their respective sectors. Where the Polish and Czechoslovak forces were to be thrown in the Hungarian General Staff was not told. During 1949 and early 1950 the Hungarian Army was built up with dazzling speed. The last acts in its socialization and reinforcement were the change in supreme war command of its field forces and the purge of its strategic leadership in 1950. Supreme war command of the field forces was transferred to the commander of the infantry (land forces), the post I had at the beginning of 1950. In March, however, the post was abolished and Colonel General Farkas, the minister of defense himself, took over the supreme war command. I was transferred to command the War (General Staff) Academy. This reassignment turned out to be a blessing in disguise, for in June all the generals in strategic positions were purged (Generals László Sólyom, chief of the General Staff; Gusztáv Illy, chief of personnel; István Beleznay, commander of the First Army Corps; Kálmán Révay, commander of the Armored Troops; György Pórffy, commander of the Artillery; Surgeon General Gusztáv Merényi-Scholtz, and Colonel Sándor Lőrinc, the general staff's chief financial officer). All of them were supplanted by party cadres lacking adequate professional training and experience, but this was of no matter since by then the Soviet advisers were completely familiar with the Hungarian environment and could supply professional leadership. All the nominal Hungarian commanders had to do was sign the advisers' orders. Everything was ready for the signal to start the war.

When the Korean war broke out, the East Central European armies were poised to strike against Yugoslavia. Had the United States and the United Nations not resisted in the Far East, that is, if the conquest of South Korea had gone unopposed, it is obvious that war would have begun in the Balkans. United Nations resistance in Korea made it likely that an attack on Yugoslavia would also have been opposed, a risk Stalin was unwilling to run. Western intervention in the Far East averted an attack on Yugoslavia by its fellow socialist states.

The preparedness of the armies of East Central Europe was at its peak during 1950 and 1951 and then fell off less precipitately than they had originally been brought to battle readiness. Once war with Yugoslavia was out, large armed forces in the satellite countries lost their *raison d'être*. The strength of the Hungarian Army, like the others in East Central Europe, was reduced substantially between 1951 and 1956 and further cuts were planned for 1956. A disproportionately large number of trained professional officers faced transfer to civilian jobs, which because of their lack of civilian skills would be less lucrative than their military positions. Many of them envisaged becoming mechanics, collective farmworkers, handimen and the like, and army morale sagged accordingly. These officers were deeply affected by the by-then widespread discontent with Soviet control and domestic totalitarian despotism. Highly demoralized, many of them were drawn to the reformers under Imre Nagy, who had already begun openly to criticize the regime, at first in undertones, then more and more forthrightly.

* * *

The military leadership of the Revolution confronted a number of pressing tasks. The existing armed forces had to be made loyal to the revolutionary government and unreliable units disbanded. The groups of freedom-fighters, which had formed spontaneously and already proved their fighting mettle, had to be incorporated. The new force, the National Guard of Hungary, was to stand by the government of revolutionary Hungary and protect it. To bring all this about, the Revolution set up new institutions.

One such as the Revolutionary Council of National Defense (RCND), created at a convention of accredited representatives of the larger freedom-fighter groups and revolutionary elements from the People's Army and the regular police. The convention had been working clandestinely in the police headquarters building on Deák

Square in the heart of Budapest. On the night of October 29/30 I headed a delegation to the prime minister to present him with the convention's resolutions. Nagy received us in the presence of former President Zoltán Tildy and the Budapest commissioner for food, Zoltán Vass. Nagy welcomed the establishment of the RCND and immediately issued a communiqué that was broadcast over Radio Kossuth in Budapest: "The RCND will recruit the new defense forces from units that have taken part in revolutionary combat, army and police units, and workers' and youth organizations. It is to reestablish domestic peace in the fatherland and insure the conditions in which the government's program announced on October 28 and 30 can be put into effect. The RCND will continue to act until a new government elected by universal suffrage and secret ballot has been sworn in. . . . Imre Nagy, chairman of the Council of Ministers of the People's Republic of Hungary."[3]

The RCND had been founded by those who had brought about the Revolution and endorsed by Imre Nagy and his government, whose prestige was respected and authority accepted by the vast majority of the nation. The source of the RCND's authority was thus twofold: the Revolution and the state. Under this double aegis, the RCND worked around the clock with the single aim of organizing Hungary's armed forces, old and new, into an institution loyal to Nagy, his government and the Hungarian nation.[4]

The Revolutionary Committee for the Defense of the Hungarian Republic (RCDHR) was set up by a congress of accredited representatives of the revolutionary organizations in the People's Army. They charged it with the direction and control of the People's Army, which they renamed *Honvéd*, the Hungarian Army's traditional title which the Stalinist regime had scrapped. Before concluding in the small hours of October 31,[5] the congress elected both officers and men of the People's Army, police officers and freedom-fighters to the RCDHR, carefully including representatives from distant parts of the country, from all branches of the People's Army, and from combat as well as supply units. Both in its inception and its membership the RCDHR was manifestly democratic, representing all branches and levels of the uniformed services.

The RCDHR was well aware of the role the army could play during the period of consolidation. It had no doubt where the sympathies of the junior officers and men of the People's Army lay. They would definitely not collaborate with a Stalinist counterrevolution, should it occur. It was equally clear, however, that many general and staff officers were inimical to the Revolution. If consolidation proceeded normally, the latter would not be able to use the army for Stalinist counterrevolutionary designs but they could certainly delay consolidation by acts of sabotage. The foremost task of the RCDHR was therefore to rid the upper echelons of military command of these Stalinist senior officers. In fact, the RCDHR had issued its first directives to this end even before the congress that set it up was over. They expelled four leading Stalinists from the army: Major General Lajos Tóth, first deputy minister of defense and chief of staff, Major Generals Jenő Hazai and Ferenc Hidvégi, both deputy directors of the main political department in the ministry of defense, and Lieutenant General István Szabó, deputy minister of defense.[6]

At my suggestion Imre Nagy authorized establishment of the Army Screening Commission (ASC). It had two responsibilities. The first was to cashier dyed-in-the-wool Stalinists, not for vengeance but because it was essential to relieve incorrigibles from duty. The second task was to review the cases of officers who had served long and with distinction in the People's Army only to be purged by the Stalinist leadership. The ASC was to be under my supervision in my capacity as chairman of the RCND. With the approval of the prime minister three senior officers were named to the ASC to begin work at once. One was a general who had never been purged and had remained on duty when the revolution broke out. Both the others were colonels who had been purged, one of whom had been rehabilitated and begun a civilian job before the Revolution, and the other had only recently been released from prison after a long term. All three were officers who had had very different experiences at the hands of the Stalinists but were highly educated and respected men whose judgment would have been accepted by broad sectors of the officer corps. The first session of the ASC was set for November 5 but never took place because of the Soviet attack. The ASC needs to be mentioned, however, to give a full picture of the organizational work that would have tranformed the army into a disciplined shield of the revolutionary regime, had it not been interrupted by the Soviet aggression.[7]

The new all-inclusive armed force of the Revolution was the National Guard of Hungary, which integrated the spontaneously formed freedom-fighter groups with the units of the army and police who had thrown their lot in with them. Consolidation of the National Guard presented a number of problems, political, psychological and technical.

Above all, the freedom fighters were highly suspicious of all those they did not know in person or who had not fought at their side.

They feared having the fruits of victory snatched from them by political machinations. By its very nature the Stalinist system had imbued many Hungarians with a great mistrust of their neighbors. The work of consolidation and the organizational efforts of the central leadership of the National Guard had therefore to be handled with kid gloves.

There were complicating psychological factors, too. The freedom-fighters were easy prey to rumors of saboteurs in hiding, Stalinist counterrevolutionary activity and so forth. The gravest result of this state of mind was the so-called Battle of the Ministry of Foreign Affairs. Late in the afternoon of November 2 a company of freedom-fighters from Hay Square (Széna tér), a stronghold in the center of Buda, the area of the capital lying on the west bank of the Danube, attacked the foreign ministry after hearing that it had been seized by agents of the Stalinist State Security Policy (AVH). Barely had they entered the building than firing broke out, each side assuming the other to be hostile. As soon as news of the "battle" was received, the building was surrounded by military and freedom-fighter tank and artillery units under my command, although we still had no clear idea what was happening in the ministry. Gradually those inside realized that they had been encircled by friendly troops under their commander in chief and the melee stopped. Providentially there had been no fatalities. When the "attackers" from Buda were lined up, a man was found in their midst in the uniform of a lieutenant colonel. Not even an officer, as it turned out, he and a couple of companions had instigated the attack and were arrested. Afterwards I explained to the rest of the men how they had let themselves be duped by counterrevolutionaries. This fearsome mistake, which had caused an interruption of cable exchange between the Hungarian foreign ministry and the United Nations while it lasted, was a telling demonstration of counterrevolutionary tactics.

A major effort was launched on October 28 to complete the consolidation of the National Guard. The initiative was taken, as it had been many times during the Revolution, by the young people. On that day the Revolutionary Committee of University Students issued a manifesto to the young people of Hungary, which said in part: "Hungarian revolutionaries! The government has fulfilled the demands of revolutionary youth. The Soviet troops are going to withdraw. The preservation of public order will be in the charge of the National Guard consisting of soldiers, policemen, students and workers. Revolutionary fighters, join the National Guard!"[8]

Similar announcements were broadcast over the radio, printed in the press, read out at meetings and disseminated by every means possible. Organizing the National Guard became a popular effort that aimed to rally the largest possible number of persons loyal to the revolution in a single force. Most of the revolutionary organizations took a hand in the task, including the Petőfi Circle, the Hungarian Writers' Association, the Musicians' Association, the Creative Artists' Association and the National Federation of Journalists. These intellectuals' organizations set up a recruiting center in Loránd Eötvös University in Budapest. The workers', police and agrarian organizations also looked to the National Guard as the defender of the Revolution and lent all the assistance they could to consolidating it.

The key task was to set up an effective central leadership for the National Guard. In an amazingly short time this was accomplished and the headquarters became a smoothly functioning group. It included representatives of the major freedom-fighter groups, who sent their best men to join its staff, reliable General Staff officers from the army, police officers, university students and workers' delegates, all of whom worked together efficiently and in heartwarming harmony.

Foes and simplistic friends of the Revolution alike have found common ground in alleging that the secret of the freedom-fighters' success was that a very able underground had prepared the Revolution and led it to success. Nothing could be further from the truth. No one had planned the Revolution in advance because nobody wanted bloodshed. Most of the population longed for fundamental changes, but through evolution, not revolution. True, Imre Nagy and his earlier "New Course" had become rallying points for the reformers. It is also true that scholars, politicians, military men, even party officials had made common cause with Nagy, but openly, not clandestinely. Nagy's program was not the secret plan of a cabal. Its intrinsic appeal and the trust Hungarians felt for Nagy were far more magnetic than any underground group could ever have been. The Hungarians were pressing for reforms not for revolution.

It might be asked, then, how the revolutionary organizations including the central staff of the National Guard were consolidated so rapidly in the face of such overwhelming odds. The main cohesive force was the quite extraordinary community of ideas the Hungarians shared in 1956. Nor should it be forgotten that during the Stalinist era everyone from all levels of society received intensive military and even guerrilla training.

Consolidation of the major freedom-fighter groups into the National Guard and organization of its central headquarters were complete by October 31. That day the RCND issued a manifesto which I signed. Printed in the daily newspapers and broadcast over Radio Kossuth, it clearly defined the status and goals of the National Guard. In part it proclaimed: "The National Guardsmen are the successors of the heroic National Guardsmen of the glorious revolution and struggle for freedom of 1848. They are thus the successors and followers of those heroic National Guardsmen who smashed the forces of aggression at the victorious battles of Ozora and Pákozd and in the spring campaign of 1849. National Guardsmen, soldiers, policemen, comrades in arms! Strengthen your battle readiness for the defense of our sacred fatherland and of the achievements of our national and democratic revolution and for the final consolidation of the revolutionary order. By disciplined behavior, further the fame that you have already achieved."[9]

That same day the RCND convention elected me as commander in chief of the National Guard and Colonel Sándor Kopácsi, the Budapest chief of police, as my deputy. Our appointments were announced in another manifesto, which proclaimed the determination of the National Guard: "Until democratic elections have been held, with all our strength we will help the consolidation of civic order and faithfully carry out the government's orders to crush any attempts at restoration [of the Stalinist regime] and any reactionary moves. The strike [begun in protest against Soviet aggression] does serious harm to the country's combat readiness. We therefore appeal for an immediate end to the strike and a return to productive work and, once work has been resumed, we urge National Guard units to keep their equipment at the ready and to remain on standby to join battle against the aggressors in case of a new attack."[10]

The military leadership's two final tasks in securing the loyalty of the armed forces to Imre Nagy's revolutionary government were to dissolve the AVH and to integrate the Frontier Guards with the new forces. The AVH was the most hated organization the communists ever imported from the Soviet Union. There was not a single program put forward by any social group in the country during the Revolution that did not call for disbandment of the AVH. As soon as the armistice was announced on October 28, Imre Nagy pledged that the AVH would be abolished without delay. The very next day the ministry of the interior put his promise into effect. An announcement declared: "The minister of justice has dissolved all police organizations with special rights. The AVH has been disbanded because such an organization is unnecessary in our democratic system."[11] This was the end of the instrument of the Stalinists' reign of terror.

Although they were under the supervision of the AVH, the Frontier Guards were a different case, a fact acknowledged by the government and people as readily as by the Frontier Guards themselves. They issued a declaration of loyalty as early as midnight on October 29: "The Frontier Guards of the Hungarian People's Republic sincerely support the Hungarian people's splendid struggle waged for our national existence and for the reestablishment of our total freedom and independence. . . . We identify ourselves with the democratic revolution."[12] This pronouncement was accepted at face value and on November 3 Imre Nagy announced their integration with the army.

The Frontier Guards were all too soon able to demonstrate their loyalty to the Revolution. When the Soviet Union started its second, invincible attack, a mass exodus from the country of more than 200,000 people began. They voted with their feet against the new, Soviet-imposed regime and against Soviet domination of Hungary. The Frontier Guards would have had no difficulty in stopping the refugees and keeping them inside the Iron Curtain, but they did not do so. Instead they helped them cross the Austrian and Yugoslav borders. By doing so, they showed that they, too, were freedom-fighters, ready to render any service to the nation in its time of disaster.

In the first phase of the Revolution, up to the armistice of October 28, the day was carried by unknown freedom-fighters whose struggle was spontaneous and without central coordination. They enjoyed the succor and support of all levels of Hungarian society with the exception of a handful of Stalinists. In the second phase, after October 28, the baton was passed to the organizers. They, too, strove to the utmost of their ability to consolidate the gains already achieved. The gallantry of the freedom-fighters and the selfless devotion of the organizers had led by the beginning of November to the remarkable internal stability of the Imre Nagy government and the efficient functioning of the new revolutionary institutions. Without doubt, the Stalinists had not been destroyed by then, only ousted from power. Some of them chose to flee abroad, mostly to the Soviet Union. Most of them simply went underground. Before the Soviet Union renewed its aggression, they tried to stir up trouble, disorder, unrest, but time and again their counterrevolutionary efforts, as at the "Battle of the Ministry of Foreign Affairs," were frustrated. There was no power that could challenge the authority of

Imre Nagy's government inside Hungary. It had to come from out-side. It was the socialist Great Power, the Soviet Union, that crushed the democratic socialist government of Hungary. Why did the Soviet Union attack Hungary? For three reasons at least.

1. The Soviet military, still under Marshal Georgi K. Zhukov, de-manded the control of Hungary as a site for missile bases. Soviet ordnance in 1956 contained only intermediate ballistic missiles, which could reach certain southern European strategic targets only if deployed in Hungary. We know that Zhukov threatened to resign if Hungary was not reoccupied as a site for Soviet missiles.

2. The residual strength of the Stalinists in the Soviet Politburo could still prevail over the rest and pressed through acceptance of the idea that an anti-Soviet chain reaction would be the inevitable consequence of letting democratic socialists stay in power in Buda-pest. Nikita S. Khrushchev confessed in a 1957 speech at the Csepel ironworks, south of Budapest, that in a prolonged debate in the Soviet Politburo before November 4 the majority initially opposed military measures in Hungary.

3. The Chinese communists, still allied with the Soviet Union, urged the Kremlin to suppress the Hungarian revolutionary govern-ment lest a global disintegration of the communist camp occur. The exchange of mutually denunciatory letters by the Chinese and Soviet communist leaders in the early 1960s contains a letter in which the Chinese claim that they were the ones who prevailed over "the So-viet revisionists" to give "aid to the Hungarian proletariat."

Whatever the main reason, in the early morning hours of Novem-ber 4 Soviet aggression resumed.

Nagy's government did not want war with the Soviet Union, not even a defensive one. There was only a linear defense perimeter around Budapest for observation and to secure the government a few hours' or, at best, days' delay in case of attack. The soldiers and freedom-fighters manning it had been forcefully instructed not to fire on Soviet troops except in an ultimate emergency; to avoid giving the Soviet troops any pretext for interference, these orders had been emphasized continually. When the massive Soviet offensive began in earnest on November 4, the defenders needed a specific, dramatic command that it was all-out war and to act accordingly.

As commander of the freedom-fighters and chairman of the RCND, I advised Nagy that the only way to make our troops aware of the real situation was for him or me to announce over Radio Kossuth that we were at war with the Soviet Union.

Imre Nagy forbade me to make such an announcement and made it clear that no such statement would be forthcoming from the civilian government either. "Ambassador [Yuri] Andropov is with me," he told me over the telephone, "and assures me there's been some mistake and the Soviet government did not order an attack on Hungary. The ambassador and I are trying to call Moscow." Moscow, of course, never answered the phone.

When I informed Nagy a little later on that same morning that there had been a major break in the Budapest defenses and that a Soviet column was nearing the Parliament building, where he had his office, he told me with a note of despair: "I don't need any more reports."

A few minutes later his voice came emotionally over Radio Kossuth: "At dawn this morning Soviet troops launched an attack on our capital city with the obvious intention of overthrowing the lawful, democratic Hungarian government. Our troops are in action."[13]

"Our troops are in action," Imre Nagy told the nation and the world, yet to his commander in chief he had said, "I don't need any more reports." There is a glaring discrepancy between these two remarks—but only at first sight.

Nagy wanted no more reports from me because the obvious consequence of any new data on the Soviet advance would have been the need to order the Hungarians either to fight or to lay down their arms. The fact of a state of war between two socialist countries could no longer be disregarded. But Nagy could not in good conscience give any combat orders. The ruins of Budapest after the siege at the end of the Second World War were still too vivid a memory, and a war with the Soviet Union would have been vain bloodshed anyhow. By affirming that Hungarian troops were in action, Nagy neither encouraged us to fight nor advised us to lay down our arms. Too much treachery had been committed in recent Hungarian history against men who had surrendered in good faith. Imre Nagy could not acquiesce in war. Instead, he left it to history to pass judgment on the socialist state that has the dubious honor of being the first to have made war on another socialist state.

NOTES

1. The author has expounded this thesis in several articles published in various journals on the twentieth anniversary of the revolution. Among them: "The First War between Socialist States," *Canadian-American Review of Hungarian Studies* (Kingston, Ont.), III, No. 2 (Fall 1976), 10-18; "Budapest 20 Years Ago," *The New York Times*, October 23, 1976; "Prima guerra fra com-

munisti," *Il Giornale* (Milan), October 23, 1976; "Az első háború szocialista országok között" [The First War between Socialist States], *Irodalmi Ujság* [Literary Gazette] (Paris), XXVII, No. 9-10 (September-October 1976). See also the thesis broadly stated in Kai Hermann, "Der Aufstand," *Stern*, No. 47, 1976.

2. The most recent account of this process is Péter Gosztony, *Zur Geschichte der europäischen Volksarmeen* (Bonn-Bad Godesberg, n.d.)

3. *A magyar forradalom és szabadságharc a hazai rádióadások tükörében 1956 október 23-november 9* [The Hungarian Revolution and Fight for Freedom in the Mirror of Domestic Radio Broadcasts, October 23-November 9] (New York, 1957) [quoted hereafter as *HRRB*], pp. 186-187. For further details, see my article "The Organization of National Defense during the Hungarian Revolution," *The Central European Federalist* (New York), XIV, No. 1 (July 1966), 6-16.

4. The organization of the staff of the RCND was quite pragmatic. Since the headquarters had to be made effective as quickly as possible, the only criteria for enlistment were revolutionary loyalty and organizational ability. It is noteworthy that students of the Revolution in Hungary have adduced statistics trying to prove the steady elimination of members of the People's Army from the staff. János Molnár, *Ellenforradalom Magyarországon 1956-ban (A polgári magyarázatok birálata)* [Counterrevolution in Hungary in 1956 (A Critique of Bourgeois Interpretations)] (Budapest, 1967), pp. 195-196.

5. *HRRB*, p. 212.

6. *HRRB*, p. 244.

7. *Az ellenforradalmi erők a magyar októberi eseményekben* [The Forces of Counterrevolution in the Hungarian October Events], 4 vols. (Budapest, 1957), III, 70.

8. *HRRB*, pp. 108, 110.

9. *HRRB*, pp. 255-256.

10. *HRRB*, pp. 340-341.

11. *HRRB*, p. 145.

12. *HRRB*, pp. 153-154.

13. *HRRB*, p. 362.

Tibor Méray

THE TRIAL OF IMRE NAGY

The execution of Imre Nagy, the prime minister of Hungary during the Revolution of 1956 and three of his associates was announced simultaneously by Radio Budapest and Radio Moscow during the night of June 16/17, 1956. After the initial shock, indignation and mourning, the mind should and we indeed do look for a rational explanation. Why did they have to die? To whose advantage was their death and whose interest did it serve? Whose will prevailed? And why did it happen precisely at that moment?

The announcement of the execution was the first official word about Imre Nagy in more than eighteen months. The last statement had been that of Grigore Preoteasa, the Rumanian foreign minister, to the United Nations General Assembly on December 3, 1956. He had informed the assembly that his government had granted asylum to Nagy and his colleagues at the request of the Hungarian government. He added: "The Rumanian government has given assurances that the group's stay in Rumania will be in accordance with all the rules of hospitality. . . . The Rumanian government has vouched that it will heed the international rules of political asylum. . . . I can state that the persons in question are grateful to the Rumanian government for the hospitality that is being offered them. I can likewise convey to you that . . . the attitude of Mr. Imre Nagy and his group is distinguished by understanding and good humor."[1]

The world had learned the circumstances in which Imre Nagy and his colleagues had been moved to Rumania. It was known that a written safe-conduct had induced them on November 23, 1956, to leave the Yugoslav embassy in Budapest, where they had taken refuge on November 4, as the Soviet intervention in Hungary had resumed. The safe-conduct had guaranteed that they could return peacefully to their homes, but scarcely had they left the embassy compound than they were seized by Soviet troops and deported to the domain of Gheorghe Gheorghiu-Dej.[2] To this day no details have ever been released about their return to Hungary. There has certainly been no statement to the effect that they were ever stripped of their safe-conducts or had renounced them of their own free will.

Nor was there ever advance word of their trial, with the exception of public assurances that none was planned. On November 26, 1956, János Kádár, the first secretary of the Hungarian Socialist Workers' Party, stated over Radio Budapest: "We have promised not to make Imre Nagy and his friends stand trial for their past crimes, even if they themselves confess to them later."[3] A spokesman for the Hungarian ministry of foreign affairs reiterated in Budapest on February 27, 1957, that the Hungarian government "has no intention of bringing Imre Nagy to trial."[4] On April 4, 1957, Kádár assured foreign correspondents that there would be no Imre Nagy trial because of the delicacy of the situation.[5] When some recalcitrant Stalinist members of the party leadership insisted that it was "unfair" to punish only the "nameless" participants in the revolution while the "main culprits" went scot-free,[6] Kádár answered at a meeting of the Central Committee in March 1958: "When a Nagy trial would have been appropriate, we weren't strong enough; now we have the strength, but it would be inopportune."[7]

Kádár's response was fair comment on domestic circumstances in Hungary in 1958 when bringing Nagy to trial could have served no useful purpose. After the bloody lessons of 1956, who would have dreamed of starting a new revolution or any other sort of action? Hungary had been engulfed by a wave of terror at the end of 1956 and in 1957. Though the exact number of its victims will probably never be revealed, Hungarian public opinion has it that several thousand were executed and at least 30,000 jailed. No further intimidation was needed to keep the country cowed. Besides, Imre Nagy and his colleagues were living in Rumania, completely isolated from the outside world, and posed no conceivable threat to the regime. Even the West had completely forgotten them. When a selection of Nagy's essays was published in several languages in 1957,[8] the Kremlinologists scarcely gave them a second glance. Only now have they begun to realize that the currently fashionable thesis of Eurocommunism was to be found in what Nagy committed to paper more than two decades ago.

No special Hungarian domestic reason for Nagy's trial and execution is apparent. Might it have been Kádár's personal thirst for vengeance? This he could easily have satisfied, for he was the undisputed leader of the party in Hungary, but there is no evidence for such a supposition nor would it have been in character. If there was no local cause, then the reason for what happened must be sought in international politics, more particularly, in international communist politics and the relations among the parties.

It must be conceded in advance that, even after twenty years, one is still obliged to speculate, because communist archival material is kept jealously secret. So many parts of this dreadful puzzle have been revealed, however, that it would be hard to make a fundamental mistake in trying to piece together the general picture. It must also be stated that, perhaps because of Hungary's smallness and its relatively "liberal" regime, it seems harder to keep a secret there than in other places under communist rule. Thus certain basic facts about the trial and what led up to it have come to light in Hungary. Contrary to conjecture that he was tried in the Soviet Union and to German press reports that he was assassinated in Rumania, it is now known that Imre Nagy was brought to trial in Budapest in the central prison on Main Street (Fő utca).[9] Despite official pronouncements, it is also known now that the four men sentenced to death (Nagy, Major General Pál Maléter, József Szilágyi and Miklós Gimes), were not tried and executed at the same time. József Szilágyi, Nagy's secretary, resisted his inquisitors and was put to death during interrogation. The fifth victim, Minister of State Géza Losonczy, notwithstanding the official version, did not die of ill health; he went on a hunger strike and was strangled under the pretext of forced feeding. These and some other tragic facts are known. What the oral chronicles of Hugary are silent about is why the trials and executions took place and on whose orders.

For the international communist movement late 1957 and the first half of 1958 were halcyon days. It was the time of the launching of the first sputnik, the period of "overtaking" America. The communist movement was stronger and more united than it had been even under Stalin. Representatives of all the communist parties of the world converged on Moscow to celebrate the fortieth anniversary of the Bolshevik revolution. Mao Tse-tung came, and representatives of the reconciled League of Communists of Yugoslavia put in their first appearance since they had been expelled from the Cominform back in 1948. Nikita Khrushchev was at the pinnacle of his power as secretary general of the Communist Party of the Soviet

Union after earlier in the year successfully sidelining his potential rivals Georgi Malenkov, Vyacheslav Molotov and Lazar Kaganovich.

It was all a charade. At the end of the great conclave the Yugoslavs declined to sign the final communiqué. This temporary disappointment was amply made up for by the fact that Mao himself had insisted that the communist camp needed a leading power and "this leading power is the Soviet Union."[10] The flattering epithet, however, only papered over a whole series of conflicts and barely hidden contradictory intentions. It became more and more clear to Khrushchev that, if, according to Mao, the Soviet Union was to be the head of the movement, China intended to be the neck that was to move the head. Part of the dispute was ideological, such as the assessment of Stalin. The Chinese considered the criticism of Stalin at the Soviet party's twentieth congress both exaggerated and fallacious.[11] Other sources of friction were more pragmatic considerations, such as the supply of atomic secrets to China and future relations with the West, including the possibility of a third world war. In Mao's view war with the West was not only inevitable but also almost desirable since, if a third or a half of mankind were to be wiped out, capitalism would be destroyed and the world would be ruled by the socialist camp.[12] Khrushchev and his associates, on the other hand, wanted to prepare for an extended period of peaceful coexistence. Mao's attitude horrified them and they wondered at equipping him with atomic arms. Later, indeed, they reneged on their commitment to do so.[13] For the time being, however, they could not afford a public confrontation with him because they were indebted to him in a number of ways. When Malenkov's group was being eliminated, they had leaned on Mao for support. And it was Mao's China that had sent Chou Enlai on an East European tour in January 1957 to restore Moscow's prestige, which had been badly damaged in the eyes of the satellites by the events in Poland and Hungary in the fall of 1956.

Thus it was that the question of the Hungarian revolution became involved in the ever more intense Sino-Soviet dispute, not as a major cause but as a side issue of no mean significance. It is true that China took a sympathetic view of the Hungarian Revolution in its early days. The first time it criticized the Soviet Union for "great-power chauvinism" was in fact over the Hungarian and Polish events.[14] By the same token China was quicker to change its attitude than even Moscow. By October 31, 1956, Peking was already calling for forceful intervention in Hungary, though not so in Poland. Later it was to accuse the Russians of having "hesitated when faced with the Hungarian rebellion,"[15] and to claim that its stand was why the Soviet

Union finally crushed the Revolution. (The claim was an overstatement, for the Soviet assault of November 4, 1956, was certainly not solely the result of China's reaction.)[16]

The Chinese claim, however, had to bring home to Khrushchev that Peking considered him a vacillating weakling, a man who lacked the basic prerequisite and merits of a true communist. He must have pondered how he could prove that he was the opposite of what he appeared to be to Peking and his East European vassals. The most obvious way would have been to have marched in step with Mao toward a third world war in the fury of which, by Mao's own calculations, between 900 million and 1,350 million persons would have perished, but for this he did not have the stomach. It seemed to him that it would be simpler, less costly and, above all, quite safe to take "strong-willed" action "worthy of a true communist" like trying and executing Imre Nagy and his associates.

There was one snag, however: Moscow's relations with Belgrade. Yugoslavia was not one of the Great Powers but Khrushchev did not consider Soviet-Yugoslav relations a secondary matter. It was Khrushchev, after all, who had initiated reconciliation with Josip Tito—and incurred China's wrath in doing so. Soviet-Yugoslav relations had generally developed well ever since Khrushchev had gone to Canossa by visiting Belgrade in May 1955, so well, in fact, that on November 2, 1956, Khrushchev had personally consulted Tito on the armed intervention in Hungary planned for November 4. If recent Yugoslav data are to be trusted, not only did Tito not object to the project but it was also he who recommended forming a Hungarian "worker-peasant" government and naming Kádár to head the postrevolutionary regime.[17] The abduction of Imre Nagy and his associates on the doorstep of the Yugoslav embassy in Budapest three weeks later elicited a protest from the Yugoslav government but it was not to be taken too seriously. Yugoslavia's participation in the world communist conference in Moscow in 1957 was evidence of that. The Yugoslavs' refusal to sign the final conference communiqué, however, had caused Khrushchev a serious loss of face and for that retaliation was due. Bringing Nagy to trial would thus kill two birds with one stone: it would show the Chinese how tough Khrushchev was and demonstrate his outrage to the Yugoslavs, who, after all, had given Nagy and his associates temporary asylum in their embassy in Budapest. Scarcely two months after the Moscow conference, on January 28, 1958, Nagy and his colleagues were indicted by the state prosecutor of Budapest. The trial on the basis of that indictment began on February 6.

Almost at once it was stopped for unknown reasons and new evidence was ordered collected.[18] It seems that Khrushchev was very reluctant to acquiesce in the failure of his Yugoslav policy. Rather than let it happen, he made a new conciliatory effort. This is indicated by János Kádár's sudden visit to Tito in late March, during which he renewed the solemn pledge that Imre Nagy and his friends would not be prosecuted. The visit had fatal consequences, however. During it Tito tried to persuade Kádár that he should emulate the line then being taken by the Poles and try to make himself a little less dependent on Moscow. Kádár wasted no time in reporting Tito's advice to Moscow.[19]

Khrushchev was not notable for his moderation and self-discipline. It is very likely that he was outraged by Kádár's report. He must have realized that, while the purpose of his conciliatory policy was to lure Yugoslavia back into the fold, Tito was just as intently bent on the opposite, on detaching the people's democracies from Soviet tutelage. In a speech in Moscow in April 1958 Khrushchev commended Kádár for disclosing Tito's intentions, for not "trying to sit astride two horses at once" by attempting to establish good relations with both East and West, as he implied Tito was doing. In another address, to the congress of the Bulgarian Communist Party in Sofia on June 3, 1958, Khrushchev went further by attacking Yugoslavia openly. Among other charges he asserted: "During the putsch [sic] in Budapest, the Yugoslav embassy became the seat of those who launched the struggle against the Hungarian People's Democracy. The embassy gave asylum to the defeatist, treacherous Imre Nagy-Losonczy group."[20]

Thereafter the fate of the "defeatists and traitors" was sealed. Nine days later the trial that had been adjourned in February had been resumed and two weeks after Khrushchev's Sofia speech, in slavish obedience to Moscow's dictates, those who had not already died in captivity were executed.

If a political prisoner is usually a tool in the hands of his captors, in a totalitarian system he is completely at the mercy of the regime. In the trial and execution of Imre Nagy and his associates, however, there was an extra facet. The added dimension in this tragic story was something entirely new and unprecedented in the history of political trials in the communist world. Imre Nagy, as has been indicated, was Nikita Khrushchev's victim. He was the victim of Khrushchev's difficulties with the Chinese and the Yugoslavs. He was the victim of Khrushchev's temperament which, while he was by no means the worst among Soviet leaders, sometimes assumed such primitive extremes as when he took off his shoe in the General Assembly of the United Nations and pounded the rostrum with it. But Imre Nagy was not simply the victim of one man's violence or derangement, nor the victim solely of circumstance. He was not even a mere victim but rather an active, creative man fulfilling a historical destiny that he himself shaped, accepted and even brought to a head.

A comparison of the documents of the Imre Nagy trial[21] with those of the show trials of the Stalin era immediately reveals a fundamental difference between them. Without exception Stalinist indictments were baseless. In good Stalinist tradition, so too were some of the charges in the Nagy trial: the "conspiracy" to seize power, the "coooperation with certain imperialist circles, above all, the American imperialists" and with Radio Free Europe. But a substantial part of the indictments in the Nagy case was true. It is true that there was an armed Revolution in Hungary; it is true that the goal of that Revolution was to achieve national independence and democracy; it is true that Imre Nagy and his associates stood at the head of that Revolution; it is true that Nagy proclaimed Hungary's neutrality and withdrawal from the Warsaw Pact. In terms of communist orthodoxy, or better, according to the norms of Soviet imperialism, Imre Nagy was without doubt guilty. Nagy intended to realize a series of reforms that Soviet imperialism would not tolerate. He intended to achieve national sovereignty and national self-determination. He intended to hold free elections. While safeguarding the postwar land reform and the socialization of basic industries, Nagy introduced popular government on the basis of socialism. Nagy's trial may be described in part as the last of the typical Stalinist great political show trials, in that the charges were replete with falsities, but it was at the same time the first major political trial of the post-Stalin era, since it prosecuted real and active opposition to totalitarian communism.

Khrushchev, who personally unmasked Stalin's unlawful actions at the Soviet party's twentieth congress and proffered "socialist legality" instead, obviously had a clear conscience (if such was necessary) that no "innocents" were sent to the gallows in the Imre Nagy case. Yet it is he who has the dubious distinction of being the communist leader who ordered the last political trial to date in Europe that ended in execution.

There is another equally significant difference between the Imre Nagy trial and the classic Stalinist show trials, a difference that relates not to the accusers but to the accused. After the horrific "preparations" to which they were subjected, the defendants in the

Stalinist trials acknowledged all the supposititious charges on which they were accused and maintained the silence expected of them about their personal achievements in the communist movement. Imre Nagy outspokenly repudiated all the fabricated offenses in his indictment and proudly owned to everything that he did do. So did the others in his boat, which was why Losonczy and Szilágyi had to die during interrogation and why Maléter and Gimes both paid the capital penalty with Nagy.

During Nagy's sojourn in the Yugoslav embassy and Rumania, Kádár's agents and Rumanian officials tried to negotiate with him. Had he been willing to exercise "self-criticism," he was offered both his freedom and high office in the Kádár regime.[22] The bargaining was to no avail. Though the trial was secret, the communiqué issued afterwards had to admit that the main defendants denied their guilt. The white book[23] the regime published later shows that Nagy, as well as disavowing wrongdoing, insisted with pride and without misgiving on the justice of his policies and those of the Revolution. The politician who had in the past faltered or temporized or gone astray thus emerged as a statesman of national and international stature. The defenseless prey of a system beyond his control and incomparably more powerful than he acquired the mantle of a hero who consciously acceded to his fate and by his martyrdom was elevated above his executioners for all time.

Exactly ten years after his execution the few sentences Imre Nagy uttered when allowed his last words were brought to the West. In their dramatic brevity these words illumine his whole career and stand as the most vivid evidence of his acceptance of his fatal destiny:

> Twice I have tried to save the honor of socialism in the Danube basin—in 1953[24] and in 1956. It was Rákosi[25] and the Russians who prevented it.
>
> If now my life is to be sacrificed to prove that all communists are not enemies of the people, I offer it willingly. After all that has happened, it has no value any longer.
>
> I realize that there will be another Imre Nagy trial at which I shall be rehabilitated and three times as many people will come to my re-interment as went to Rajk's.[26] My only dread is that my eulogy will be given by those who betrayed me.[27]

NOTES

1. *La vérité sur l'affaire Nagy: Les faits, les documents, les témoignages internationaux*, pref. by Albert Camus (Paris, [1958]), pp. 16-17.

2. The Yugoslav government note to the Hungarian government quoted by G. Altman in *Magyar Szó* [Hungarian Voice] (Novi Sad), November 25, 1956.

3. Radio Budapest, November 26, 1956.

4. Tibor Méray, *Imre Nagy, l'homme trahi* (Paris, 1960), p. 325.

5. Ibid.

6. Károly Kiss's speech of February 15, 1957. Ibid., p. 324. Antal Apró's speech of February 20, 1957. *La vérité* . . . , p. 28. József Révai in *Népszabadság* [People's Freedom] (Budapest), March 7, 1957. All three party leaders were Stalinists: Kiss was speaker of the National Assembly, Apró headed the trade-union movement, and Révai was the chief ideologist and one of the top four men in the party (together with Mátyás Rákosi, Ernő Gerő and Mihály Farkas).

7. While this statement by Kádár has never been published, it has been circulating ever since it was uttered in a way that indicates that it was an inspired leak from Kádár's inner circle.

8. Imre Nagy, *On Communism: In Defense of the New Course* (New York and London, 1957).

9. Kádár's personal statement to the French journalist André Fontaine, quoted in *Le Monde* (Paris), February 19, 1964.

10. Mao's speech to Moscow University students in November 1957. Méray, *La rupture Moucou-Pékin* (Paris, 1966), p. 41.

11. See "The Historical Experiences of the Dictatorship of the Proletariat," *Jen-min jih-pao* [People's Daily] (Peking), April 5, 1956. This commentary was published shortly after the twentieth congress of the Communist Party of the Soviet Union.

12. Mao's speech in Moscow on November 17, 1957. Méray, *La rupture*. . . , p. 46.

13. *Jen-min jih-pao*, September 3, 1956.

14. Ibid., various articles published between October 25 and October 31, 1956.

15. "The Dispute between the Leadership of the Communist Party of the Soviet Union and Ourselves: Its Origins and Evolution," ibid., September 6, 1963.

16. For an analysis of the Soviet intervention in Hungary, see Méray, *Imre Nagy* . . . , pp. 253-262.

17. Zvonko Staubringer, "Tito's Historical Opposition to Stalinism," *Vjesnik* [Courier] (Zagreb), April 26, 1976.

18. The pause coincided with Kádár's statement to the party Central Committee about the inopportuneness of trying Nagy. See n. 7.

19. Méray, *Imre Nagy* . . . , pp. 328-329. The incident was widely reported in the Western press under both Moscow and Belgrade datelines. Cf. Khrushchev's remarks in Sofia and Moscow.

20. Ibid., p. 331.

21. The indictment and verdict published after the trial are in *La vérité* . . . , pp. 35 ff.

22. Kumara P. S. Menon, India's ambassador to Moscow, Warsaw and Budapest from 1952 to 1961, reported that, when taking leave of Kádár, the Hungarian had told him that Nagy had been urged to sign a statement that he no longer considered himself the head of government. Had he done so, his life would have been spared, but Nagy refused. Menon, *The Flying Troika: Extracts from a Diary* (Bombay, London & New York, 1963), p. 305, quoted in Méray, *That Day in Budapest* (New York, 1969), pp. 464-465.

23. *Imre Nagy és bűntársai ellenforradalmi összeesküvése* [The Counterrevolutionary Conspiracy of Imre Nagy and His Accomplices] (Budapest, [1958]).

24. During his first ministry from June 1953 to April 1955, Nagy introduced a series of liberal reforms which included the rehabilitation of János Kádár, who had been serving a long prison term on spurious charges.

25. Mátyás Rákosi, Stalinist first secretary of the Hungarian communist party from 1940 to July 1956 and an inveterate foe of Nagy.

26. László Rajk, a leading communist, former interior minister and foreign minister, was arrested in 1949. At a classic show trial he admitted to all the false charges against him and was sentenced to death by hanging as a Titoist agent. He was rehabilitated posthumously in March 1956. Tens of thousands attended the ceremonies in Budapest when the party had him and three associates reinterred with honor on October 6, 1956.

27. *Irodalmi Újság* [Literary Gazette] (Paris), June 1-5, 1968.

PART II
THE REVOLUTION AND HUNGARY'S NEIGHBORS

Andrey A. Amalrik

LETTER TO THE EDITOR

Utrecht
April 12, 1977

Dear Professor Király:

Forgive me for not answering your letter of February 1977 for so long. I kept hoping that I would be able to fulfill your request, but my travels in Europe and teaching assignments at Utrecht University have left me no time for it. Therefore I will only briefly answer your question and you can simply publish my letter in your book, if it has not yet come out.

I think that the Hungarian Revolution of 1956 was a turning point in the history of the communist bloc. It did not bring about—nor could it have brought about—the collapse of the bloc or the liberation of Hungary, but it clearly indicated that two courses of resistance exist. The first is national opposition to dominant Soviet communism. Such heterogeneous phenomena as the national communism of Rumania, the liberal national movement in Slovakia in 1967-1968, the rising of national feeling within the Soviet Union as well as "Eurocommunism"—all would have been equally impossible without the Hungarian example.

The other course is social resistance. Neither the "Prague Spring" nor the Polish workers' disturbances nor the human rights movement in the Soviet Union could have happened without the Hungarian Revolution of 1956.

Thus, when I speak of a turning point, I have in mind the change from passive acceptance of things as they are and feelings of despair to comprehension that the world can and will alter, even though it will require many years and enormous sacrifice. It is already possible to say that many of the sacrifices have not been in vain. For Hungary now enjoys the greatest freedom of any country in East Central Europe precisely because the Hungarians demonstrated their ability to resist with weapons in hand. Although the revolution was suppressed, the communist powers cannot but remember this lesson.

The events of 1956, which culminated in the Hungarian Revolution, left a deep impression on me and many my age. It is with good reason that we call ourselves the generation of 1956. On everything that we have done and will do lies and will lie the imprint of that heroic year.

I wish you well.

Yours,

(Signed) Andrey A. Amalrik

Adam Bromke

POLAND

The Hungarian Revolution of 1956 had a profound impact upon Poland. One reason for this was, of course, that the upheaval in Hungary coincided with Poland's "peaceful revolution" of the same year. The Poles watched the Hungarians' struggle with great interest and with immense sympathy. Probably nowhere else in the world did the Hungarian Revolution evoke at first so much spontaneous support, and, when it was all over, such genuine sorrow, as in Poland.

It was during a Hungarian demonstration of solidarity with the Poles on October 23, 1956—symbolically conducted in front of the statue of the Polish hero of the Hungarian Revolution of 1848-1849, General Józef Bem—that the initial fighting in Budapest broke out. The Poles warmly reciprocated the Hungarians' sentiments and throughout the revolution repeatedly demonstrated their solidarity with the Hungarian "freedom fighters".

The press in Poland covered the events in Hungary extensively and faithfully. On October 28 the Polish communist party daily, *Trybuna ludu* [People's Tribune] declared that the source of the Hungarian tragedy "should not be sought in a simplified version of 'alien agencies', nor in looking for counterrevolution at every turn. . . . It should be sought primarily in the errors, distortions and even crimes of the former Stalinist period". On the same day the party's Central Committee issued an appeal addressed to "[our] Hungarian brothers" urging them to stop the shedding of fraternal blood. Personal accounts of the battle in Budapest were published in the two popular weeklies, *Po prostu* [In Plain Words] and *Nowa kultura* [New Culture] , and were widely read throughout the country.

Money, clothing and medical supplies were openly collected in Poland and it was from that country that the first plane carrying blood plasma arrived in Budapest. Youth rallies in sympathy with the Hungarians were held in various Polish cities. On November 2 a manifesto issued by the Central Committee of the Polish United Workers' Party accurately described the Polish attitude. "The Polish nation," it declared, "follows the course of events in Hungary with great emotion." Indeed, after the second Soviet intervention in Hungary, emotions in Poland were so intense that there was a distinct danger of a popular explosion. On November 7 Radio Warsaw reported that the situation in the country had "reached boiling point" and appealed for calm.

The Poles supported the Hungarians until the very bitter end. Even after the uprising was crushed, the Polish communist party clung to its own interpretation of the events in Hungary. It was over that issue that Poland took a step unprecedented for a member country of the Soviet bloc. On November 21, 1956, in the General Assembly vote on the admission of United Nations' observers to Hungary, the Poles did not support the Soviet Union but instead joined the Yugoslavs in abstention.

The suppression of Hungary was such a highly emotional issue in Poland that even in the spring of 1958, when the execution of Imre Nagy was announced, party First Secretary Władysław Gomułka still displayed great caution. His comments on the subject were the last to be delivered by an East Central European communist leader and were couched in carefully measured terms. Speaking in Gdańsk on June 28 Gomułka acknowledged the event but detached himself from it. "It is not up to us," he said, "to appraise the scope of the guilt and the justice of the punishment of the defendants in the Nagy trial. This is an internal Hungarian matter."

* * *

After the events of 1956 one question was often posed: why did the Soviet Union intervene in Hungary but refrain from similar action in Poland? The standard answer became that, in contrast to the Poles, the Hungarians had gone too far, particularly in striving to restore the multiparty system and to embrace neutrality. The events in Czechoslovakia in 1968, however, confounded this explanation. The Czechs and the Slovaks attempted neither to overthrow communist party rule nor to withdraw from the Warsaw Pact, yet they suffered the same fate as the Hungarians.

The fact is that it is still not known what triggers Soviet intervention in the various East Central European countries. As a Polish writer, Marek Tarniewski, put it recently: "Russia's alarm reaction is difficult to anticipate; just now it is sporadic, but it always can happen and occasionally does happen, often over the most unlikely matters." The Eastern Europeans must always be conscious of Soviet presence. It is dangerous for a small country, the Polish author observes, whenever "a revolutionary situation occurs within its borders that does not coincide with the revolutionary situation outside. First the Hungarians, and then the Czechs and the Slovaks, had to learn this lesson."

Yet, Tarniewski adds, the reality of the Soviet presence in East Central Europe does not preclude all political change there. The mechanism of intervention is a delicate one and precisely what triggers it is probably not known even in Moscow. Rather, decisions are arrived at on the basis of the evidence available in each specific case. They are affected by the constellation of political forces in the USSR and their perception of the situation in the international scene. The Soviet Union's alarm reaction, Tarniewski concludes, "can be adjusted; . . . it depends on the specific circumstances existing in each country."[1]

The respective domestic situations in Hungary and Poland in 1956, as the Russians correctly perceived, were in many ways different. The Stalinist system in Hungary had been more repressive than in Poland and produced correspondingly stronger reaction. In Poland the alternative communist leadership under Gomułka had been permitted gradually to take over, while in Hungary First Secretary Mátyás Rákosi's persistent efforts to stay in power had undermined Imre Nagy and produced a more explosive situation. In the final analysis, however, probably the major difference between the two nations was the differing perceptions of their respective situation in the international sphere in 1956.

For Hungary the experience of the Second World War was less traumatic than for Poland. On the one hand, the Hungarians did not play a major political and military role in it, trying instead to weather the storm as best they could. Their losses were less extensive than those of the Poles. They failed to win back their pre-1918 territory, but at least they retained that of 1938. On the other hand, though the Hungarians had historically experienced periods of accommodation with the Austrians and the Germans, dealing with the Russians was for them a novel experience. In short, the Hungarians were, relative to the Poles, internally stronger and they found Moscow's suzerainty over their country less tolerable.

In contrast, the Second World War marked a major watershed in Poland's history. From beginning to end the Polish question stood at the very center of wartime diplomacy and the Polish military contribution to the Allied side was considerable. The relative losses which Poland suffered during the war were second to none. The Poles thus were understandably embittered at the West for not helping them to preserve their independence from Moscow. They suffered sizable territorial losses in the east and the compensation they were given in the west aggravated tension with Germany. In these circumstances it was natural that the Poles embraced political realism and reverted to a stance they had already tried out in the nineteenth century, namely, seeking an accommodation with Russia.[2]

* * *

It is within the context of the specific historical phase through which they were passing in 1956 that the Hungarian Revolution acquired a very special, one might say almost personal, significance for the Poles. There is no question that for a good many of them watching the battle in Budapest was a deep emotional experience—as if they themselves were taking part in it. There were several reasons why the Poles projected themselves in this fashion into the Hungarian scene.

First of all, the Poles and the Hungarians have been traditionally tied together by firm bonds of friendship. It is one of those rare situations in Europe where the two peoples genuinely like each other. Hungarian-Polish friendship has not been rooted in common interest— and perhaps for this reason it has been even stronger. In fact, on various occasions in the past—as, for instance, during the Second World War—the Poles and the Hungarians have found themselves in opposite camps, yet even then their mutual sympathy has been preserved and they have tried to help each other as best they could.

The friendship between the two nations goes back to their early history when several Hungarian kings occupied the Polish throne and Polish princes wore St. Stephen's crown. It was consolidated through the centuries of common struggle against the Turks. In more recent times, during the revolution of 1848-1849, many Poles fought on the Hungarian side against the Austrians and the Russians. It was while serving under General Józef Bem that the great Hungarian poet, Sándor Petőfi, fell in battle. The close personal ties, especially among the aristocratic circles in the two countries, resulted in somewhat similar styles of life and, despite the major linguistic difference, a distinct cultural affinity still exists between the two peoples. No Pole feels quite alien in Budapest and probably no Hungarian is out of place in Kraków. Thus it is easy for each people to understand the emotions and to appreciate the actions, especially when directed against foreign power, of the other.

The battle of Budapest of 1956 appealed to the Poles' imagination even more because it reminded them so vividly of the Warsaw uprising of 1944. Indeed, there were strong similarities between these two historic episodes, In both cases a handful of freedom-fighters waged a desperate struggle against overwhelming odds and without any outside assistance. While watching the newsreels of the Hungarian uprising in 1956, many Poles must have relived their own—at that time still relatively recent—experience.

Yet it was precisely the traumatic shock of the defeat in Warsaw in 1944 which, more than anything else, made the Poles abandon their all-out struggle for freedom and embrace political realism. While watching the lonely Hungarian Revolution, then, the Poles' reaction must have been ambivalent and in some respects even contradictory. With their hearts they were with the Budapest freedom-fighters, but reason cautioned them against joining the "Hungarian brothers." In the end, though caution prevailed, it was certainly contrary to the Poles' own impulses and, in fact, it resulted in the Poles finding their own stance not to their liking. Their sentiments were articulated by Polish poet Adam Ważyk, who, writing in *Nowa kultura* on November 25, 1956, sadly observed: "We used to be the conscience of history but now our silence has become *raison d'état.*"

When it was all over in Hungary, the Poles mourned, but the ambivalence of their feelings was nevertheless eased. They knew that, by joining the Hungarians in the battle against the Russians, they would not have saved Budapest and they would have exposed Warsaw—once again—to a similar fate. They still admired the Hungarians for "acting like Poles," yet at the same time congratulated themselves for "acting like Czechs." In short, the outcome of the Hungarian Revolution was to convince the Polish people that their course of not counting on the assistance of the West and of striving for a *modus vivendi* with the Soviet Union was correct.

Paradoxically, it was the January 1957 issue of the communist theoretical monthly *Nowe drogi* [New Roads] —trying to make political capital for the then badly shaken Polish United Workers'

Party—which accurately summed up the situation. "Let us remember," it declared, "that at the time of the Hungarian tragedy the foreign radio stations appealed to the Poles for reason and restraint. Those reactionary forces in Poland which would like to spread disorder ought to know that the Americans are extremely reluctant to shed their own blood."

The realist posture paid off for Poland. The "peaceful revolution" of 1956 brought about important changes in the country: the abandonment of the collectivization of agriculture, a marked improvement of the Roman Catholic church's position and the expansion of intellectual freedom. By the late 1950s Poland was by far the freest country in the communist bloc.

* * *

The defeat of the revolution in 1956, it seems, had a similar effect in Hungary to what the crushing of the Warsaw uprising in 1944 had in Poland. It resulted in the abandonment of an all-out struggle for freedom and the adoption of political realism. When in the early 1960s, after the initial period of repression, First Secretary János Kádár offered the Hungarians a possibility of accommodation with the Soviet Union, they eagerly embraced it. Moscow's suzerainty was accepted in exchange for a modicum of domestic freedom. The compromise served the Hungarians well. In a few years the situation in the country improved markedly. In fact, it soon became better than that in Poland. Toward the end of the 1960s Hungary, in turn, was the freest and one of the most prosperous countries in East Central Europe.

The *modus vivendi* with Moscow, however, also had its price. The communist system has become entrenched and the very man who betrayed the revolution of 1956, János Kádár, has stayed at the helm. In foreign policy Hungary has followed the Soviet Union at every turn. During the Czechoslovak crisis of 1968 the Hungarians acted even worse "than Czechs"; they helped the Russians—together with the Poles—to invade their neighbor, which was striving to free itself from Moscow's suzerainty.

There is no reason to believe that the Hungarians like their realistic posture any more now than the Poles liked theirs in 1956. Yet the memories of the defeat of their revolution are still strong enough to prevent them from moving away from it. The Hungarians' thoroughgoing realism was described by a participant in the 1956 uprising presently living in the West, Charles Fenyvesi: "The West will not lift a finger and it is madness to think that we can bring a real change. Heroism is dead. . . . One makes a separate peace with the regime. The arrangement is comfortable, cozy. The trouble is that it stinks."[3]

It is ironic that, as the Hungarians embraced political realism, the Poles moved in the opposite direction. In the 1960s, as the defeatist memories of the Second World War faded, popular pressure steadily mounted in Poland. When Gomułka steered away from a program of reforms, he encountered strong opposition. Intellectual ferment once again gathered momentum and in 1968 the students took to the streets. In 1970 Gomułka, the hero of Poland's "peaceful revolution" of 1956, was overthrown by rioting workers and replaced by Edward Gierek. When in the mid-1970s Gierek in turn tried to move away from a program of reform, he found himself faced with the united opposition of the workers, the intellectuals and the Catholic church. The workers' riots in Radom and Ursus in June 1976 brought the country to the verge of a revolution and threw the communist party once again into a retreat.[4]

In the 1970s Poland has thus caught up and in some respects even surpassed Hungary. In the economic sphere the Hungarians still remain ahead of the Poles; in the realm of intellectual freedom the Poles are more or less at par with the Hungarians, while the scope of religious freedom is greater by far in Poland than in Hungary. Both countries maintain broad contacts with the West, although the Poles are somewhat bolder in elevating them to the level of formal diplomatic relations.

Despite different approaches, there are considerable similarities between Hungary and Poland today. They occupy a unique position in the Soviet orbit. In the domestic sphere they are the two freest countries in Eastern Europe; in this regard they are by now ahead even of Yugoslavia. They are still subject to overall Soviet suzerainty and, given their geographic position, there is little prospect that this will change soon, but the communist systems in both countries have already been largely "domesticated." Evidently, the tactic of oscillating between idealism and realism, at times resorting to pressure and at times to compromise, has served the two nations well.

NOTES

1. Marek Tarniewski, *Ewolucja czy rewolucja* [Evolution or Revolution] (Paris, 1974), pp. 69, 272.

2. For an extensive treatment of this subject see Adam Bromke, *Poland's Politics: Idealism vs. Realism* (Cambridge, Mass., 1967).

3. "Hungary 20 Years Later," *The New York Times Magazine*, October 17, 1976.

4. The events in Poland in the last decade are discussed in Adam Bromke, "Poland's Political Crisis", *The World Today*, March 1969; "Beyond the Gomułka Era", *Foreign Affairs*, April 1971; "Poland Under Gierek, A New Political Style", *Problems of Communism*, September 1972; "A New Juncture in Poland", *Problems of Communism*, September 1976; and also in Adam Bromke and John W. Strong, eds., *Gierek's Poland* (New York, 1973).

Stephen Fischer-Galați

RUMANIA

An assessment of the impact of the Hungarian Revolution of 1956 on Rumania is conditioned by a set of assumptions concerning Rumania in 1956 and 1976. If it is assumed, as it has been at one time or another by students of Rumanian affairs, that relations between Hungary and Rumania have been either fraternal or hostile at all times since the establishment of the respective people's republics in the forties and that therefore the Hungarian Revolution could not have affected the basic character of these relations, there would be no reason to entertain the subject at all. This would also be true if it were assumed, as others have done, that the Rumanian "independent course" evolved only after 1956 and that its origins and development were essentially unrelated to the revolution. However, since I hold views somewhat different from those mentioned on both the Rumanian independent course and Rumanian-Hungarian relations, I shall attempt to assess the character and significance of the impact of the revolution of 1956 in Hungary on the history of Rumanian communism and of communist Rumania during the twenty years that have elapsed since the memorable events of 1956.[1]

In October 1956 the principal problem that faced the leaders of Rumania was political survival. The threat to Gheorghe Gheorghiu-Dej's security came from Moscow rather than from the revolutionary potential of discontented workers, students, intellectuals, peasants or national minorities. Nikita Khrushchev sought Gheorghiu-Dej's removal from power from as early as 1954 and the execution of Lucrețiu Pătrășcanu and the conviction of Vasile Luca in that self-same year were symptomatic of the fears of the Rumanian communist leadership.[2] Gheorghiu-Dej's rapprochement with Josip Tito which culminated in Gheorghiu's visit to Belgrade in the very month of the

Hungarian Revolution was designed to secure Moscow's recognition of Rumania's right to construct its own road to socialism on the basis of the objective conditions prevailing in Rumania at that time. In October 1956 Gheorghiu-Dej claimed that as a proven Rumanian leader he was best able to appraise those conditions. There was no implication in Gheorghiu-Dej's assessment that Rumanian communism or communism in Rumania were threatened by non-Rumanian elements within the party, state or population at large, but there was a presumption that a majority of the population of Rumania, whether Rumanian or not, was insufficiently mature politically—in other words, it was too anticommunist—to warrant adoption of Titoist, Khrushchevite or other unsuitable models within Rumania proper.[3]

The Hungarian Revolution merely confirmed the accuracy of Gheorghiu-Dej's assessment of conditions in Rumania and in effect allowed consolidation of his potentially tenuous position in the country itself and *vis-à-vis* Moscow. The Hungarian Revolution raised several issues critical to Gheorghiu-Dej. The first was that of acceptance of communist rule in Rumania by Rumanians and Hungarians alike. The several manifestations of unrest evident among workers, students and intellectuals outside Transylvania were as important to Gheorghiu-Dej as the specifically pro-Hungarian manifestations that occurred among the Magyar population in Transylvania proper.[4] Although it was expedient to condemn the Magyar "counterrevolutionaries" in Rumania as disloyal by virtue of their being Hungarian, the fact was that the pro-Hungarian demonstrations that occurred in Transylvania were not so much manifestations of Hungarian nationalism as of pure anticommunism. Yet the Hungarian demonstrations in their anticommunist forms offered Gheorghiu-Dej the opportunity to restate the validity of his analysis of the party and state apparatus in Transylvania all the more vigorously. Perhaps of even greater concern to Gheorghiu-Dej than the anticommunist manifestations in Transylvania was the utilization by the Kremlin of Soviet armed forces stationed in Rumania in the military operations directed against the revolutionaries in Hungary. It is true that Gheorghiu-Dej supported the Soviet intervention at a time of potential threat to his own regime but this is not to say that he failed to realize that the utilization of troops for securing Moscow's continuing control over the satellites set a potentially dangerous precedent. The securing of his own position in Rumania and by extension a degree of autonomy for Rumania *vis-à-vis* the USSR was adjudged, in the wake of the

Hungarian Revolution, to require correction of such adverse factors as a bad economy, continuing Soviet military presence and nonidentification of the nation with the party.[5] As is generally known, however, the search for security was unsuccessful because of the Kremlin's opposition to allowing consolidation of Gheorghiu-Dej's power within the framework of a specific "Rumanian road to socialism." The formal rejection by Moscow in December 1956 of Rumania's political demands, which would have facilitated the attainment of limited autonomy, brought the lessons of 1956 into sharper focus and ushered in postrevolutionary reaction to the Hungarian Revolution in both the USSR and Rumania.[6]

A clear delineation of the outline of Rumania's so-called "independent course" became evident in 1957. The impact of the Hungarian Revolution was also evident in several respects. First, the Rumanians exploited the contradictions within the socialist camp, related in part to Moscow's actions during the revolution, particularly those focusing on relations between Moscow and Peking. In essence Gheorghiu-Dej embraced the Chinese position favoring the maintenance of communist orthodoxy within sovereign communist nation states. The Rumanian course could be justified in these terms.[7] Second, and distinctly related to the events of 1956, was the exploitation by Gheorghiu-Dej of Khrushchev's need to restore "peaceful coexistence" with the West. Internecine struggles within the Kremlin, which ultimately resulted in the exclusion of the "antiparty" group from power in the summer of 1957, provided additional opportunities for the attainment of Gheorghiu-Dej's immediate goal of securing the removal of Soviet armed forces from Rumania. The withdrawal of the troops in 1958 as a result of a complicated triple power play involving Khrushchev's relations with China, the West and the leadership of his own party was followed by the formulation of plans for Rumania's multilateral economic development on a basis contrary to that envisaged by its partners in Comecon and by a massive ideological campaign designed to equate the interest of the Rumanian people with those of the Rumanian Communist Party and the Rumanian historic tradition with that of the Rumanian communist state.[8] These actions which shaped Rumania's independent course invited opposition from Moscow and fellow members of the bloc and inevitably led to reaffirmation of the tenets of historic Rumanian nationalism directed against the traditional enemies of Rumania's historic aspirations, Russia and Hungary.

The main source of opposition to the attainment of Gheorghiu-Dej's goals was Moscow but the main scapegoats in Rumania were the Hungarians of Transylvania. The alleged chauvinism manifested by intellectuals and other Magyar inhabitants of Transylvania provided the rationale for the *de facto* abolition of the Hungarian Bólyai University in Cluj in 1959 and its incorporation into a unitary Babeş-Bolyai University, dominated by Rumanian cadres, and the reorganization and de-Magyarization in 1960 of the Magyar Autonomous Region, originally established in 1950.[9] By 1964 the Rumanization of the university and of the once homogenous Magyar region was in full swing and Transylvania itself reassumed the unenviable traditional position of a political football in international and intra-Rumanian-Hungarian relations.

It remains a matter of speculation whether the reopening of the Transylvanian question in the context of territorial revisionism was provoked by Rumanian nationalist actions directed against the Hungarian minority or whether it was the leadership of the Soviet Union that sought to undercut Rumania's self-proclaimed independent course from Comecon and general bloc policies favored by the Kremlin by encouraging and supporting anti-Rumanian manifestations by Magyar elements in Transylvania and, at least tacitly, by anti-Rumanian forces in Budapest.[10] The assumption that the reopening of the Bessarabian question in 1964 by Gheorghiu-Dej and Mao Tse-tung, with corollary attacks by the Chinese against Soviet territorial imperialism in East Central Europe, brought on a riposte from Khrushchev via Budapest is probably accurate.[11] However, conditions doubtless caused by massive Rumanization of Magyar enclaves in Transylvania as part of the socialist transformation of Rumania into a Rumanian communist state. In the sixties the polemic was essentially restricted to arguments focusing on Rumania's historic rights to Transylvania.[12] János Kádár's regime pursued a policy of extreme caution in its tacit support of the rights of conationals in Transylvania and of the irredentist positions expounded by Magyar historians. Budapest was also infinitely less vocal in its support of anti-Rumanian positions adopted by its partners in Comecon, most notably by the USSR, the German Democratic Republic and Czechoslovakia, and, in general, kept a low profile in the growing conflict between Moscow and Bucharest over the extent to which Nicolae Ceauşescu could successfully complete the legacy of Gheorghiu-Dej in the quest for Rumanian independence.[13] However, after the Soviet invasion of Czechoslovakia and the ensuing years of threaten-

ed Soviet military action against dissidents, Budapest collaborated
with Moscow in overt anti-Rumanian moves primarily through joint
military maneuvers on Hungary's borders with Rumania and also by
endorsing anti-Rumanian positions in Comecon and by supporting
the validity of the Brezhnev doctrine as it pertained to Rumania.[14]
It is also fair to say that Budapest had become increasingly more
active in voicing concern over the fate of the Magyar population in
Transylvania in the face of the ever rising nationalist fervor displayed by the Ceauşescu regime. In fact, at the twenty-fifth congress of the Communist Party of the Soviet Union in 1976, Kádár
himself restated Hungary's displeasure over Rumania's treatment
of the Magyar population by implicitly approving the doctrine of
"1,000 years" enunciated by nationalist Hungarian historians and
publicists.[15] Kádár's statements were most probably made with the
Kremlin's approval, if not at its behest, at a time of continuing conflict between Bucharest and Moscow over a variety of issues, not the
least of which was that of Rumanian rights to Bessarabia and northern Bukovina.

In any event, the Rumanian offensive against the historic position
of the Magyar population in Transylvania has gained in intensity in the
1970s as Ceauşescu's independent Rumanian course has assumed increasingly more virulent nationalist forms with specific anti-Hungarian
overtones. Paradoxically, the current anti-Rumanian—or at least pro-
Hungarian—attitudes displayed by the Magyar population of Transylvania are not necessarily reactions to the nationalist excesses of
the Bucharest regime or expressions of sympathy toward Kádár's
Hungary. Rather, they reflect the general dissatisfaction shared by
most inhabitants of Rumania with the economic, social and cultural
policies of the Ceauşescu regime. The ever more pervasive socialist
nationalism identified with the rule of Ceauşescu in Rumania is contrasted, and not only by Hungarians, with the more moderate and
more viable formulae for governance expounded and practiced by
Kádár in Hungary. In the absence of the preferred options that appeared to be momentarily available in October 1956, the current
Hungarian road to socialism seems worthy of emulation in Rumania
to Magyars and to many non-Magyars alike. That image of Kádár's
Hungary and of the realities of Hungarian communism has been
countered by Bucharest in terms of Rumania's own historic and
communist experience. The reaction, of necessity anti-Magyar in
character, has entailed *inter alia* restrictions of contacts between
Transylvania's Hungarians and the Magyar population of Hungary
proper.[16] Budapest's and Moscow's response to these Rumanian

policies has been to encourage anti-Rumanian manifestations by Hungarian nationalist groups throughout the world.[17]

The old and the new wounds inflicted upon Magyars and Rumanians by nationalism and communism have been reopened after the cures prescribed by Joseph Stalin proved to be worse than the disease. The Hungarian Revolution of 1956 was symptomatic of the disease. The cures prescribed by the Rumanian leadership after 1956 differed considerably from those prescribed by Moscow and by Budapest. All have evidently been inappropriate. Even the most recent manifestations of outward Rumanian-Hungarian friendship, which have become evident since Ceauşescu's visit to the Soviet Union in the summer of 1976 and Leonid Brezhnev's return visit of a few months later, do not truly mask the reality of continuing tensions between Rumania and Hungary, tensions that can be attributed in no small measure to the "objective historic conditions" which were renewed and exacerbated by the Hungarian Revolution of 1956 and which were subsequently exploited by the Kremlin, by Bucharest and by Budapest to the detriment of all concerned.

NOTES

1. For varying interpretations see Kenneth Jowitt, *Revolutionary Breakthroughs and National Development: The Case of Romania, 1944-1965* (Berkeley, 1971); Ghiţa Ionescu, *Communism in Rumania 1944-1962* (London and New York, 1964); Trond Gilberg, *Modernization in Romania Since World War II* (New York and London, 1975); Stephen Fischer-Galaţi, *The New Rumania: From People's Democracy to Socialist Republic* (Cambridge, Mass., 1967) and *Twentieth Century Rumania* (New York, 1970).

2. A carefully documented analysis of these events and of their implications is in Fischer-Galaţi, *The New Rumania*, pp. 44-62.

3. Gheorghe Gheorghiu-Dej, *Raportul de activate al comitetului central al Partidului Muncitoresc Romîn la congresul al II-lea al partidului* [Report of the Central Committee of the Rumanian Workers' Party at the Second Party Congress] (Bucureşti, 1956), pp. 5-160. A convenient summary of the proceedings of the second congress is in Ionescu, *op. cit.*, pp. 240-247.

4. A perceptive and informative discussion of these conditions and their significance is in *ibid.*, pp. 262-273.

5. See especially Fischer-Galaţi, *The New Rumania*, pp. 63-64.

6. The divergences between Moscow and Bucharest are clearly illustrated in the joint declaration on the Soviet-Rumanian negotiations held in Moscow between November 26 and December 3, 1956, published in an English version in *Soviet News* (Moscow), December 4, 1956.

7. The evolution of Gheorghiu-Dej's attitudes and policies becomes most apparent from analyzing the contents of several major speeches delivered between the December 1956 plenum of the party's Central Committee and the

plenum of June 28-July 3, 1957. These materials will be found in Gheorghe Gheorghiu-Dej, *Articole și cuvîntări, decembrie 1955-iulie 1959* [Articles and Speeches, December 1955-July 1959] (București, 1959), pp. 208-305.

8. On the evolution of the Rumanian independent course, see Fischer-Galați, *The New Rumania*, pp. 67-68.

9. Aside from materials contained in *Scînteia* (Bucharest) of July 3, 1959, and of December 25, 1960, see also the illuminating discussion of these issues by Ionescu, *op. cit.*, pp. 293-295.

10. On the political issues related to integration through Comecon see the very careful discussion by John Michael Montias, *Economic Development in Communist Rumania* (Cambridge, Mass., 1967), pp. 187-230.

11. Details, although occasionally conflicting, will be found in *The New York Times*, June 26, 1964, and July 15, 1964, and in *Scînteia* of July 15, 1964. See also Fischer-Galați, *The New Rumania*, pp. 105-107.

12. Massive polemics started in 1964 and the number of books and articles produced in both countries all directly or indirectly related to the polemics increased in proportion to the acerbity of the arguments about historic rights and corollary questions.

13. See Montias, *op. cit.*, pp. 205-230 and Fischer-Galați, *Twentieth Century Rumania*, pp. 193-200.

14. Of special interest in this connection is Ceaușescu's speech at the Helsinki Conference published and interpreted in *Revue Roumaine d'Etudes Internationales* (Bucharest), IX, 4, 30, 1975, pp. 315-324.

15. Insight into the significance of these actions may be gained from reading a major Rumanian policy statement in *Scînteia* of April 24, 1976.

16. Housing and travel restrictions were imposed in 1975 but slightly eased in the case of natives of Rumania in 1976.

17. Elaborate press manifestos and political appeals, including parades and other noisy manifestations, directed against alleged Rumanian violations of human rights have been promoted with much fanfare by militant Hungarian émigré groups in recent months. The scope of these activities apparently transcends that of normal émigré politics.

George Klein

YUGOSLAVIA

The Hungarian Revolution of 1956 represents a major watershed in the history of communism in East Central Europe. The Leninist dictum that socialist states would not go to war with each other because they did not possess a dominant bourgeois class in search of foreign markets had already been brought into serious question by the Soviet blockade of Yugoslavia during the years 1948 through 1953.[1] It was further shattered by the Hungarian Revolution of 1956. The Soviet military intervention in Hungary exposed clearly that the armed forces of a neighboring socialist state could be committed in order to maintain an unpopular regime and to serve the political and economic purposes of the invading power. The repression of demonstrations in Berlin in 1953, or the blockade of Yugoslavia, was one matter; the unleashing of the full fury of Soviet armor and artillery in one of the great cities of Europe, Budapest, was another.

Yugoslavia occupied a special position in this conflict because it had radiated influence throughout the communist bloc ever since the Second World War when Josip Tito rose to power by essentially autonomous means. Yugoslavia had maintained its independence against Soviet opposition since its expulsion from the Cominform in 1948 and this made it a beacon to all those forces within the bloc which strove to institute some form of "national communism." Partisans of an independent path to communism could be found in all the communist parties of East Central Europe, despite the fact that in Bulgaria, Czechoslovakia and the German Democratic Republic such tendencies were not permitted to surface. Yugoslavia therefore exercised a great influence over the events in Hungary. The influence of the Hungarian events on the Yugoslav polity is less demonstrable.

Between 1953 and 1956 Hungary underwent a purge of many of

the leaders who had been the most vocal critics of Yugoslav "revisionism" during the Stalinist era. János Kádár and Imre Nagy, who had once been charged with Titoism, were restored to full party membership and political respectability during this period. Others less fortunate, like László Rajk, could only be rehabilitated posthumously. The rehabilitations opened new vistas for the Yugoslav-Hungarian relationship. The Belgrade Declaration of June 1955 raised the hope that the Yugoslav position on both domestic and international issues would be generally accepted within the bloc.[2] The Hungarian Revolution shattered all such hopes.

The Hungarian events had little effect on Yugoslav internal developments. Yugoslavia had undergone five years of vilification at the hands of the Stalinist leaderships of East Central Europe and had suffered both blockade and constant military threats. As Tito had pointed out, the wounds of these events would take many years to heal. Even the overtures directed at Yugoslavia between the twentieth congress of the Communist Party of the Soviet Union and the Hungarian Revolution were received with great skepsis by both the leaders and the populace of Yugoslavia. The invective directed at Yugoslavia in the wake of the Soviet intervention in Hungary was viewed almost as a return to the normal tenor of Soviet-Yugoslav relations.

In the face of the Hungarian events the general population was apprehensive but it maintained its usual discipline in the face of Soviet threats. The mass reaction was fear mingled with hope. The fear constituted apprehension that relations would sink to the previous low level of the Stalinist era; the hope was based on expectations that even the Hungarian Revolution would not irrevocably interrupt normalization of relations. The Yugoslav press played down the crisis by the neutrality of its reports.

Yugoslavia possesses a Hungarian minority of 504,000, most of whom live in the province of Vojvodina which borders Hungary. This population remained passive as it had in all previous crises. Immediately after the Second World War the Hungarian minority had been treated with great hostility because Admiral Miklós Horthy's Hungary had been considered an enthusiastic ally of National Socialist Germany. As elsewhere in East Central Europe, the deportation of the Hungarian minority from Yugoslavia was considered in the immediate postwar years. Most Hungarians remained but there were obvious ceilings on their opportunities for political participation in a state run by a triumphant Partisan movement. The Hungarian minority was suspect during the early postwar years and its main object was to avoid the wrath of the preponderant Slav majority. After the proclamation of workers' self-management in June of 1950, the Yugoslav state moved into a far more tolerant phase. The national minorities suffered little cultural oppression and were not stifled in the overt expression of their respective cultures as long as they did not challenge the ideological tenets of the regime. The news filtering from Mátyás Rákosi's Hungary during the early 1950s was scarcely such as to encourage profound nostalgia for the Hungarian homeland. The Hungarian minority in the Vojvodina is prosperous by Yugoslav standards and enjoyed greater freedom of movement, including the visitation of relatives in Hungary, than their conationals across the border. The perceived comparisons were hardly favorable to Hungary, particularly after the decollectivization of Yugoslav agriculture in the years 1950 to 1953. A search of the literature on the Hungarian minority in Yugoslavia discloses few documented signs of hostile political activity on the part of the Hungarians. The Hungarians participate in a system which offers them rather broad opportunities for political involvement at a local level. This outlet served to blunt the edge of ethnic discontent in postwar Yugoslavia.

The situation in Hungary provided little inspiration to those nationalists who might have been inclined to identify with the neighboring homeland for reasons of patriotism. The discernible Yugoslav reaction to the Hungarian events was almost entirely on the official level. There was widespread sympathy at all levels for the suffering of the Hungarian people and Yugoslavia rendered assistance to those who filtered across the border in search of refuge, but beyond that there was almost universal apprehension lest the conflict spill across the Yugoslav border.

The Hungarian Revolution influenced Yugoslav relationships with the entire Soviet bloc rather than any internal Yugoslav development. Yugoslavia had influenced the events of October 1956 in Poland and Hungary and exercised a subterranean influence throughout East Central Europe and in the Soviet Union itself. The Yugoslav influence stemmed from its differing domestic methods of governance rather than from ideology or propaganda.

* * *

In 1953 Yugoslavia passed the Fundamental Law which replaced the Stalinist Constitution of 1946.[3] This represented the institutionalization of the major reorganizations of the government and economic institutions that had been promulgated. The resultant reforms went far beyond mere cosmetics or rhetoric. The Yugoslav reform program was essentially a reaction to the Stalinist overcentralization of economic and political institutions. Between 1953 and 1956 Yugoslavia largely abolished the cumbersome machinery for central economic planning and transferred thousands of functionaries from offices concerned with the administration of production to the enterprises themselves.[4] The Yugoslav leadership concluded that the economic reforms had to be accompanied by institutional modifications which would give local decision-makers enough scope to make the transformation of the system meaningful. These reforms set the stage for the development of a socialist market economy at a later date.

The Yugoslav reforms had been popular domestically. Once Yugoslav policy was committed to decentralization, it would have been almost impossible for the central authorities to recapture all the powers voluntarily surrendered to the republics and communes without major upheavals. This was understood by even the Soviet leadership, including the secretary general of the Communist Party of the Soviet Union, Nikita Khrushchev, and Premier Nikolai Bulganin when they landed in Belgrade in May of 1955. Their journey was undertaken in the hope of reestablishing full state and party relations between the two countries and, if possible, to coax Yugoslavia closer to the bloc position. While the visit failed in its primary intent, it legitimized polycentric communism throughout East Central Europe and had drastic effects on the stability of the bloc regimes.[5] The consequences of the Soviet-Yugoslav normalization were felt most acutely in Poland and Hungary. These two polities had opposed communization more stubbornly than the other bloc members and had therefore the most repressive governments. The discrediting of Stalin at the twentieth congress of the Communist Party of the Soviet Union accelerated the tempo of change in both states. It had the effect of legalizing the Yugoslav position and thoroughly discrediting the leaderships that had engaged in a bloody hunt for all Titoists only a few years earlier.

Poland at least possessed a surviving communist alternative to the Stalinist stalwarts in the personage of Władysław Gomułka. Gomułka managed to stabilize the situation in October of 1956 by exercising tight discipline over the Polish United Workers' Party and by enlisting the aid of the primate of the Roman Catholic Church in Poland, Stefan Cardinal Wyszyński. This united the Polish people behind the government in an unprecedented show of unity and enabled Gomułka to withstand major Soviet pressure. Hungary's Imre Nagy and József Cardinal Mindszenty did not possess the leadership qualities of their

Polish counterparts. The Nagy regime was swept along by events which it did not manage or control. In all of these events, Yugoslavia played an influential role.

Mátyás Rákosi was replaced on July 18, 1956, as first secretary of the Hungarian Workers' Party, largely to placate Tito as much as to still domestic discontent with his predecessor, Ernő Gerő, a staunch Stalinist. The appointment of Nagy accelerated the influence of the Yugoslav example within Hungary. During the summer of 1956 Hungarians in responsible leadership positions visited Yugoslavia with the expressed purpose of studying the system of workers' self-management.[6] During the summer workers' councils sprang up in a variety of Hungarian enterprises. These replaced the moribund trade unions which had served only as "transmission belts" for even the most unpopular policies. The Nagy leadership was carried along by these events and legitimized the role of the workers' councils.[7] Even the Kádár leadership did not initially propose to do away with the workers' council structure after the Soviet intervention. This attested to the general popularity of the councils. The councils played a significant role in the October and November events of 1956 in Hungary. One day before the outbreak of the revolution on October 22, the directors of the Petőfi Circle issued a manifesto to the Central Committee, the third point of which urged:

> The Central Committee and the government should adopt every means possible to insure the development of socialist democracy in Hungary.... by asserting the legitimate political aspirations of the working class, and by introducing self-management in the factories and a workers' democracy. [8]

The workers' councils organized general strikes during the crisis and generally supported the reform movement. This was particularly true in the city of Miskolc where the Borsod County workers' council called a general strike.[9] After initial lip service to the principle of workers' self-management, the Kádár regime sabotaged it almost from the beginning of its rule.

The Hungarian events proved traumatic to what remained of the Stalinist leaderships within the Soviet bloc. Yugoslavia encountered a serious backlash in the wake of the Hungarian events. This convinced the Yugoslavs more than ever to maintain their independence from the Soviet Union. They were no longer isolated internationally, as they had been in the period 1948 to 1953, and they wielded major influence in the entire nonaligned world.

The major impact of the Hungarian events on Yugoslavia took the form of unmitigated hostility from the bloc governments in place of

Khrushchev's earlier courtship. The leaders who emerged were those who had previously vilified Yugoslavia, such as Antonín Novotný and Václav Kopecký in Czechoslovakia. The orthodox leaderships tried to shift the blame for the events onto Yugoslavia and the Soviet efforts at rapprochement. The immediate reaction of these regimes was not, however, as stringent as that which developed on the eve of the seventh congress of the Yugoslav League of Communists a couple of years later.

During 1956 and 1957 the Soviet leaders in concert with other bloc leaders did not unleash their full hostility toward the Yugoslav version of communism. It was only after the consolidation in power of the Soviet-sponsored Hungarian regime that all the accumulated hostility came to full expression. The Hungarian revolution confronted the Soviet leadership with its principal nightmare, namely, the potential dissolution of the Soviet bloc. Even the Yugoslav leadership entertained few illusions about its ability to survive independent of other communist regimes in East Central Europe and gave its unqualified approval to the second Soviet intervention in Hungary.

Three specific areas of special concern to the Yugoslavs arose in the course of the Soviet intervention in Hungary. The first of these was the gradual suppression of those institutions that had been modeled on the Yugoslav example of workers' self-management. During the initial period of Kádár's power he supported the workers' councils, but once his regime was established in power, factory militia-units were built as a counterforce to the councils, which were abolished in 1959. Secondly, in the course of the fighting thousands of refugees crossed the Yugoslav border seeking asylum. Yugoslavia provided a haven for Hungarians of all political hues. Thousands of these refugees were permitted quiet exit to the West. Thirdly, the most grievous of all the incidents that strained Yugoslav relations with the Soviet Union and Hungary was the case of Imre Nagy. Nagy, who had been the spokesman for a reorganization along Yugoslav lines, took refuge in the Yugoslav embassy in Budapest after the Soviet intervention. The Yugoslavs made strenuous efforts to insure Nagy's personal safety and negotiated a safe-conduct for Nagy with the Hungarian authorities. Nagy left the Yugoslav embassy on November 22 under the assurance of the safe-conduct. As soon as a bus had carried him off the embassy grounds, he was arrested by representatives of the Soviet secret police. This gross violation of the Hungarian-Yugoslav understanding was presented to the world as a request by Nagy for asylum in Rumania.[10]

The course of the Hungarian Revolution embittered the Soviet-Yugoslav dialogue. The Soviet Union abandoned the spirit of the Belgrade Declaration and pointed out through its various East Central European spokesmen that separate roads to communism would only lead to catastrophe, as manifested by the Hungarian and Polish events. Tito defended the Yugoslav position in equally resounding terms. His "I told you so" tone, as symbolized by a speech delivered at Pula, November 11, 1956, was particularly infuriating to the bloc leaders. Tito stated:

> In some countries and parties of East Europe certain leaders are saying that this cannot happen in their lands, that they have a strong organization, a strong army, a powerful police force, and that their membership is already informed of everything, and that they will hold the whole thing firmly in their hands. This was also said by Gerö. This was also said by Rákosi. And what does it avail them now? Nothing at all if they do not change their methods and if the people rise in revolt one day. What they have sown since 1948 they are reaping now.[11]

While the Yugoslav regime did not support the later developments in the Hungarian events, it did hold out for the maintenance of a reform course in Hungary. Its motives were the preservation of a climate in which Yugoslavia could maintain its individuality. The events of 1957 and 1958 brought affairs back to the state that had existed in 1953. The Yugoslavs faced the unmitigated hostility of all the nonreform regimes within the Soviet bloc to which a new state had been added, the People's Republic of China.

The Chinese entered East Central European politics during the winter of 1955-1956 when Chou En-lai visited the Soviet Union and the East Central European states, seeking unity within the socialist camp. Chou En-lai's initial stance was not entirely unsympathetic to the reform movements in the light of Chinese experience of Soviet hegemonism.[12] It was the specter of dissolution that propelled the Chinese into backing Soviet orthodoxy after the Hungarian Revolution of 1956. Yugoslavia became the principal focus of Chinese attacks. Some analysts maintain that Yugoslavia served as a surrogate for the Soviet Union itself. To the Chinese the Yugoslav "deviation" obviously represented the most "extreme" of all the reformist tendencies which they decried throughout the bloc. Yugoslavia was in effect labeled a state that placed itself in the service of Western imperialism.[13] The stridency of the Chinese attacks matched those in evidence during the most anti-Titoist period of the Stalin era.

Relations between Yugoslavia and the rest of the Soviet bloc continued to deteriorate through 1957 and 1958. This was entirely attributable to the consequences of the Hungarian events. Tito refused to attend the fortieth anniversary of the Bolshevik revolution in Moscow after the Soviet Union and the German Democratic Republic had canceled promised credits to Yugoslavia. Tito's response to the criticism was presented in these terms:

> They now wish to shift the blame for certain important matters onto our shoulders. For example, they persistently maintain that Yugoslavia bears a large part of the blame for the events in Hungary. There is not a bit of truth in this charge. On the contrary, it was we who warned against the negative consequences of the policies carried out by the Rákosi clique, and they themselves have admitted that these policies gave rise to a very bad state of affairs. When the tragic events occurred in Hungary, bringing consequences which adversely affected the prestige of the Soviet Union throughout the world, they wished to slough off the responsibility, to put it on us.
>
> Of course we can never permit this . . . for we are not to blame. . . . We have not contributed to a single adverse development in any country.[14]

The greater tension was engendered by the draft program of the Yugoslav League of Communists which was circulated in advance of its seventh congress, to take place April 22 through 26 in Ljubljana. The opening salvo, fired by the Soviet party Central Committee's theoretical journal, *Kommunist*, on April 18, 1958, was followed up throughout the bloc. The criticisms have been summarized under the following headings:

1. Yugoslav refusal to acknowledge the "leading role" of the Soviet Party and the USSR, to copy Soviet experience and to admit Soviet liberation of the entire area after the Second World War.
2. Yugoslavia's equation of the East and West power blocs, its "underestimation" of US "imperialism" and acceptance of US aid, and its lack of appreciation of Soviet aid.
3. Yugoslav encouragement of various heresies such as revisionism of the "leading role of the party" and the theory that a strong governmental apparatus in a communist state tends to become a power in itself and should be curbed.
4. Yugoslavia's thesis that "state capitalism" may evolve into "socialism" and refusal to acknowledge the necessity of revolution for the overthrow of capitalism.
5. Yugoslav "overemphasis" on nationalism and independence, assertion of its right to propagandize its own theories outside its own borders and its denial that revolution is taking place in any countries except the USSR, China and Yugoslavia.
6. Yugoslavia's equivocal position during the Hungarian Revolution.
7. Yugoslav refusal to sign the 12-nation declaration of a "Commonwealth of Socialist States."[15]

The list of charges is familiar to all those who have studied the substance of the broadsides fired at Yugoslavia during the years of the Soviet blockade. The Soviet bloc refused to send official delegations to the seventh congress of the League of Communists of Yugoslavia. It sent unofficial observers who walked out *en masse* during a speech by Vice President Aleksandar Ranković; only the Poles remained seated. The tone of the Polish, Rumanian and Hungarian press remained relatively conciliatory compared to the more strident criticisms emanating from the rest of the bloc. Many of the leaders obviously hoped that Yugoslavia once again would be placed beyond the pale of polite communist societies.

On June 17, 1958, the execution of Imre Nagy, General Pál Maleter, József Szilágyi and Miklós Gimes were announced. This reopened the incident which was still fresh in the memory of the Yugoslav leaders. The executions were probably designed to have the same effect as was sought in the earlier trials of revisionists in the Stalin era, namely, to serve as a warning to all those who might be tempted to emulate the Yugoslavs.

The general anti-Yugoslav tenor was reinforced by Bulgaria's resurrection of the Macedonian question. Bulgarian vociferousness on the issue of Macedonia usually reflects Soviet positions on Yugoslavia. It is beyond the present scope to delve into the complexity of the issues involved in the Yugoslav-Bulgarian dispute over the status of Yugoslavia's Macedonian republic. In general, Bulgarian emphasis on the Macedonian issue fluctuates with Soviet-Yugoslav relations. Nineteen fifty-eight was a good year to renew the dispute.

The Hungarian Revolution had a profound effect on Yugoslav foreign policy. Until the Hungarian Revolution took place, there was a real possibility that Yugoslavia might find an amicable accommodation with the Soviet bloc. The Belgrade Declaration and the various economic arrangements which the Soviet Union offered to Yugoslavia might have made it very difficult for the Yugoslav regime to remain outside the bloc. There were pressures from within the Yugoslav party for such a policy. The Hungarian Revolution and the seventh party congress in 1958 discredited all pro-Soviet spokesmen. After the congress it was clear that Yugoslavia's foreign policy would be guided, as in the past, by the national interests of the country combined with *Realpolitik*. The Hungarian Revolution had only a minimal impact on internal developments in Yugoslavia. Its primary effect in domestic politics has been to keep the pro-Soviet minority silent. It has reinforced the faith of the leadership of the Yugoslav League of Communists in the correctness of the course charted in the early 1950s and maintained to the present day.

NOTES

1. V. I. Lenin, *Selected Works*, Vol. I (Moscow, 1947), pp. 718-19.

2. *Keesing's Contemporary Archives*, June 18-25, 1955, pp. 14265-66.

3. *New Fundamental Law of Yugoslavia* (Beograd, 1953).

4. Walter Hildebrandt, "Die innenpolitische Abwendung vom Stalinismus nach dem Kominformkonflikt 1948-1953,"in Werner Markert (ed.),*Jugoslawien* (Köln, 1954), p. 144.

5. Trond Gilberg, "Yugoslavia, Albania, and Eastern Europe," Chapter 6 in Charles Gati (ed.), *The International Politics of Eastern Europe* (New York, 1976), pp. 108 ff.

6. "Workers and the State: II," *East Europe*, VIII, No. 3 (March 1959),19-28.

7. Ibid.

8. Ibid.

9. Ibid.

10. *Scînteia* (Bucharest), December 6, 1956.

11. *Borba* (Belgrade), November 16, 1956, p. 1.

12. Robin Remington, "China's Emerging Role in Eastern Europe," Chapter 5 in Gati, *op. cit.*, pp. 83 ff.

13. "Through Yugoslav Eyes," *East Europe*, IX, No. 8 (August 1960), 31.

14. "Texts and Documents: Tito Speech to Socialist Alliance," *East Europe*, VI, No. 6 (June 1957), 63-64.

15. "Current Developments," *East Europe*, VII, No. 7 (July 1958), 28-33.

Paul E. Zinner

CZECHOSLOVAKIA

Did the Hungarian Revolution of 1956 have an impact on developments in Czechoslovakia, and if so, what kind of effect did it have? These seemingly simple and straightforward questions are not susceptible to easy, confident and substantiated answers. The main reason is the sparsity of documentation on which to draw for analysis and interpretation. Yet the very paucity of references to Hungary in contemporary materials and in the retrospective, memoir literature suggests that the Hungarian events of 1956 on the whole had remarkably scant influence on Czechoslovak developments.[1] Otherwise the documentation would be richer and references to Hungary would abound among source materials available in the public domain. This inference is buttressed by consultation with a small number of knowledgeable persons who have left Czechoslovakia since 1968. Their personal reminiscences do not form an adequate "scientific" sample, but they do shed light on official attitudes and on opinions and beliefs held by representative individuals in various stations in life. They are persuasive and significantly illustrative of prevailing sentiments—especially among the Czechoslovak population.

In the ensuing few pages an attempt will be made to assess what kind of effect the Hungarian Revolution had on Czechoslovak developments and to explain why the impact was severely limited, apart from stultifying incipient, mildly reformist trends in the latter part of 1956. Because of the unique evolutionary pattern of Czechoslovak politics the scope of the present inquiry extends over a considerable time span (1956-1968) that encompasses three distinct phases: a) the Hungarian Revolution and its immediate aftermath, b) the intervening years between Hungary's great historic trauma and the first overt signs of stirrings that have become popularly identified as the "Prague Spring" (approximately the turn of the year 1967-68), and c) the

tumultuous developments of 1968 up to and including the invasion
of Czechoslovakia by the military forces of the Warsaw Pact late in
August of that year.

* * *

The most significant consequence of the outbreak of revolution in
Hungary was to nip in the bud modest reformist strivings in Czecho-
slovakia and to strengthen an emerging tough, uncompromising, essentially Stalinist type of leadership headed by Antonín Novotný,
who had been elevated to the first secretaryship of the Communist
Party of Czechoslovakia in September 1953. Reformist tendencies
had been in evidence since 1953—as elsewhere in Eastern Europe.
Although they did not develop on as wide a scale as in Poland or
Hungary, they were in some particulars influenced by the "New
Course" experiment associated with the premiership of Imre Nagy,
especially as they pertained to the agricultural economy. Their
champion was Antonín Zápotocký, a venerable trade union leader
who became the country's president following the death of Klement
Gottwald in March 1953, less than a fortnight after Stalin's funeral.
Zápotocký, like Nagy, advocated an easing of pressures on the peasantry. Because of his moderation, but for other, personal reasons as
well, he came into conflict with Novotný, whose star was then rising
and who strove to secure his primacy in the party hierarchy by
undercutting his senior colleague and rival. For Zápotocký had an
established reputation among workers and enjoyed a certain degree
of popularity as a relatively decent person, somewhat akin to Mikhail
Kalinin in the Soviet Union. Like Kalinin he had a faculty for easy,
folksy communication with the masses. By contrast, Novotný was
an upstart. He had risen through the ranks of the party only after
1945 and his career, reminiscent of Stalin's ascent to power, was
that of a typical bureaucrat, a seemingly unprepossessing *apparatchik* lacking all personal charisma, but very adept at manipulating his
environment by administrative means.

Novotný won the struggle for power, in part by deftly accusing
Zápotocký of not adhering to the then much heralded style of collective leadership, thus securing the support of the Soviet leadership
in his own behalf. Their contest overshadowed and adversely affected the elaboration of a comprehensive program of reforms. On the
contrary, in the political arena Czechoslovakia was moving in a direction opposite to that of most other East Central European countries. While in Hungary and elsewhere the victims of Stalinist purge

trials were being gradually rehabilitated, in Czechoslovakia a spate of such trials took place, and only the most perfunctory lip service was paid to reviewing the verdict of the monster trial of Rudolf Slánský and others, which had taken place in November of 1952.[2] A commission appointed to review the Slánský trial failed to exonerate him. Instead, it reached the startling conclusion that he had indeed been an imperialist agent as charged, but on the model of Lavrenty P. Beria, the infamous chief of the Soviet secret police, a matter not known at the time of the trial.

The historical opportunity presented by the immediate post-Stalin period to steer the country on a steadier course and heal the wounds inflicted on the body politic in the frenzied years of Stalinist terror went unexploited. Nor was there any discernible turn for the better in 1956, in the wake of Nikita Khrushchev's revelations about Stalin's crimes and the condemnation of the cult of personality at the twentieth congress of the Communist Party of the Soviet Union. The postcongress debate in Czechoslovakia merely exacerbated the conflict between Zápotocký and Novotný and their respective supporters. Zápotocký urged the party to draw the proper conclusions from what had just transpired in Moscow, while Novotný opted essentially for a stand-pat, obstructionist, stonewalling posture. Under these circumstances, signs of progressive developments in neighboring Poland and Hungary were looked upon askance by the Czechoslovak leadership, whose efforts concentrated (not unlike First Secretary Mátyás Rákosi's in Hungary throughout the spring) on suppressing unrest and agitation.

That Novotný succeeded where Rákosi failed was due in large part to the fact that Rákosi was finally forced to admit his responsibility for killing innocent victims (including László Rajk) whereas Novotný was not so stigmatized. Whatever role he played in the Slánský trial, he was not the responsible official in charge but rather a direct beneficiary of Slánský's downfall, and that did not create the intense revulsion of feeling against him that developed in Hungary against Rákosi and ultimately caused his dismissal. In part, economic conditions in Czechoslovakia helped to mitigate some of the worst effects of political repression. The country's economy was in good shape, material needs were attended to and the workers did not have an acute sense of deprivation that might have galvanized them into political action. The maintenance of domestic order and tranquility was therefore not an insuperable task.

The reaction of the Czechoslovak authorities at the outbreak of revolution in Hungary, as might have been expected, was thoroughly inhospitable to the cause of the insurgents and supportive of the Soviet Union? Novotny not only accepted as inevitable and proper armed intervention by the Soviet Union to guard the achievements of socialism, but urged that it be undertaken expeditiously and offered troops. Under his management, Czechoslovakia, whose geographic position is that of a wedge between Hungary and Poland, effectively played the part of a buffer between these two countries, preventing any sort of joining of forces on their part, should they have shown an inclination to do so. Novotný also provided asylum for János Kádár, who, contrary to generally accepted belief, was in Prague in the crucial hours of betrayal of the revolution, readying his appeal to the Hungarian people and composing his cabinet of ministers there.

What attitudes the population had toward the unfolding drama in Hungary even now cannot be determined with pinpoint accuracy. On the whole, the regime—though jittery in the face of an unfathomable threat—did not have much difficulty in insulating the country from outside influence and in preventing revolutionary agitation from spilling over the sensitive southern border of Slovakia along which a heavy concentration of some half a million or more ethnic Hungarians live.

The presence of this national minority and the memory of Hungarian irredentism, which undoubtedly survives in the minds at least of an older generation of Czechs and Slovaks, probably accounted for a less than enthusiastic response to the events in neighboring Hungary. The authorities skillfully exploited the theme of civil and possibly international war in the event that Hungarian reactionaries won the upper hand and renewed their bid for Magyar-inhabited Slovak territory. Given the peaceable propensities of the population, the threat of violence and of its dire consequences was a telling argument at the disposal of the regime.

Another prevalent concern, voiced by the propaganda machine of the government but quite spontaneously felt by many people, especially workers and members of the communist party, regardless of their specific disposition toward the policies of their own leaders, involved the fate of socialism in Hungary. A substantial majority of the Czechoslovak population and an overwhelming number of workers favored the preservation of socialism. In the absence of reliable information about the rapidly changing political scene in Hungary and against a background of firmly entrenched prejudice against Hungary and the Hungarians—of which a general sense of that country's feudal legacy and still surviving reactionary political and social orientation was an integral part—many people were easily persuaded that at issue there was a counterrevolutionary onslaught on socialism with the aim of restoring capitalism.

The testimony of highly educated, discerning individuals, who were in an exceptionally advantageous position to monitor developments, bespeaks a growing sense of uneasiness about the turn of events in Hungary. They sympathized with, or at least were fascinated by, the early phase of the revolution, which they viewed as the destruction of the Stalinist edifice there. But after October 30 or so they experienced increasing dismay at the emergence of a multiparty structure, at what they perceived to be unmistakable evidence of the dismantling of the achievements of the past, and finally at the prospect of a Hungary outside the framework of the Warsaw Pact. Thus they did not condemn Soviet intervention, for they saw it as essential to safeguard socialism and retain Hungary in the Warsaw Pact structure. This obviated the necessity of contemplating the fortification of the southern borders of Czechoslovakia against an inimical state at a reputed expense of several billions of crowns. The opinions of people such as these were also heavily influenced by what they understood to be the views of a respected communist leader like Josip Tito of Yugoslavia. His apparent approval of the Soviet intervention convinced them that their own analysis was correct, their fears justified and the intervention justifiable. That they thought this way was a reflection of the severe limitation of their critical faculties. They were products and victims of a restrictive environment which had effectively narrowed their horizons. At best they stood at the threshold of an evolutionary process, which culminated for many of them in active participation in the "Prague Spring" some twelve years later.

*　*　*

In the course of the intervening years neither they nor the population at large gave evidence of having learned any lessons from the Hungarian Revolution. The events of 1956 were quickly forgotten and little attention was paid to the postrevolutionary rehabilitation of Hungary, the policy of "Kádárization," some aspects of which might well have been applicable to Czechoslovakia. It was not until well after the brutal suppression of the "Prague Spring" that its more prominent instigators turned to a systematic exploration of the Kádár model as possibly of relevance to Czechoslovakia.

The regime in its turn did not fail to hold its Hungarian comrades responsible for the disaster that had befallen them: the revolution and its aftermath.[4] In the view of the communist leadership "the Hungarian comrades were too lenient toward the reactionaries, too accommodating toward their critics, and gave them a chance to attack the party leadership, all of which was then exploited by the counterrevolutionary faction in an attack on the actual foundation of the people's power in Hungary."[5] The conclusions to be drawn from this analysis were obvious and the party acted accordingly. It was at pains to avoid the "mistakes" it had attributed to the Hungarians. To this end it frantically ferreted out all suspected "revisionists" and silenced all critics.

Czechoslovakia was in the throes of neo-Stalinism. The country's policies were formulated and implemented within narrow constraints that discouraged comparisons with the external, even the Soviet, environment. In their narrow, sectarian frame of mind, the Czechoslovak leaders failed to take advantage of opportunities to institute domestic reform and develop patterns of interaction with other socialist states, notably the USSR, that would enhance the country's independence. That such opportunities existed was amply demonstrated in Hungary, Poland and Rumania. Perhaps, the Czechoslovak leaders did not feel the need to take advantage of latitudes then allowed by the Kremlin. In any event, the public record is barren in regard to any continuing preoccupation with Hungary. Occasional references to that country either emphasized the differences between its socioeconomic development and that of Czechoslovakia or invoked the threat (as Novotný did in 1967) of a Hungarian type of cataclysm if the rising chorus of criticism to which he was then subjected did not subside.

The reformers themselves, who under the impetus of accumulated grievances with the performance of the regime grew more vocal and mounted an offensive against established authority, seemed oblivious of any connection between their quest for changes and the antecedents of the Hungarian Revolution of 1956.

This does not rule out the possibility that in the inner recesses of some research institutes or scientific establishments, where the reform movement was in slow gestation, the literature about the Hungarian Revolution was being read and evaluated. Evidence of familiarity with writings on the revolution, even Western works, did come to light in the course of the "Prague Spring," but it is not known how widespread such knowledge was and how well it was absorbed by those who had it. Evidence to this effect is nonexistent, so that one might surmise that, if there was any awareness of the applicability of some phases of the Hungarian developments to Czechoslovakia, such awareness was either locked deep in the minds and hearts of people or was buried in their subconscious.

* * *

As the reform movement gathered momentum and became a mighty stream dominating internal politics in Czechoslovakia, those who were caught up in it were swept away by euphoria. They, as indeed the Hungarians a dozen years earlier (with somewhat greater justification, to be sure, for they had no precedent to refer to), felt that their experiences were *sui generis* (and to a large degree, in specifics this was true). Their universe did not transcend the geographic limits and historic traditions of their country. They reveled in the rediscovery (and in the case of the young, the discovery) of past glory, heroes, values and myths that were exclusively their own. And as the processes of change continued to gather force, they gave rise to a much needed revitalization of the national spirit and badly tattered national self-esteem. Under these circumstances it would have been perhaps unrealistic to expect people to compare themselves with other nations. It was natural, though also unrealistic, that they should exaggerate their national exclusiveness and find the rationale for it not only in the intangible but also in the tangible legacies of the past, including economic structure and sociopolitical forces.

The spirit of the "Prague Spring" was well articulated by Eduard Goldstücker, chairman of the Czechoslovak Writers' Union and a leader in the reform movement:

> It can be said without the slightest hint of nationalism or exaggerated parochialism that Czechoslovakia entered the socialist phase of its historical evolution as both industrially and politically the most advanced of all the present socialist countries. When I say 'industrially,' I hope this is clear and does not require further explanation. When I say 'politically,' I mean the historical fact that the nations of our country have had the longest and strongest democratic tradition and the most direct experience with democracy, even if it was a bourgeois democracy.
> What is happening in this country today, friends, is nothing other than a process in which socialism in the Czechoslovak Socialist Republic—this inseparable component of the socialist part of the world—is molded into forms determined by the requirements of life, the traditions, and the possibilities open to our nations. I hope all of us have learned the common lesson that any disregard for these basic factors has always sooner or later had to be dearly paid for and that socialism cannot be reduced to the size of a bed that would suit only Procrustes.[6]

Right or wrong, the emphasis on uniqueness swept all other considerations aside. References to Hungary could not be found in the media. A single exception was an article by Osvald Machotka, a a member of the Institute of International Politics and Economics of the Czechoslovak Academy of Sciences, on the occasion of the tenth anniversary of the execution of Imre Nagy. Selecting observations I made about Nagy in my book *Revolution in Hungary*, Machotka seemed to warn Secretary General Alexander Dubček and his supporters not to be naïve about the perspective in which Czechoslovak developments would be seen in the Kremlin and of the reaction of the Soviet Union to these:

> The American historian [sic] P. Zinner writes . . . that Nagy was absolutely convinced that the decision [to leave the Warsaw Pact] was correct and talked enthusiastically about the Soviet Union's acceptance of a 'neutral but sincerely friendly Hungary.' 'His conviction that the Russians would agree to an independent but friendly state on Russia's borders is unbelievable,' writes Zinner. 'However, everything points to the sincerity of his convictions. Nagy's appeal to the Great Powers to guarantee Hungary's neutrality, which he made at a moment when Soviet tanks were already rolling across Hungarian territory, was an act of despair and evidence of his failure to grasp international reality.'[7]

Machotka's article infuriated the Hungarians, with whom Dubček was just then consulting. It elicited no discernible echoes in Czechoslovakia. This is not to say that by midsummer at least a few scattered individuals did not turn their attention to the possibility of a parallel between Hungary's experiences in 1956 and Czechoslovakia's in 1968, at least in so far as the Kremlin's response was concerned. The philosopher Ivan Sviták, whose thinking had outpaced that of almost everyone else in the country, became preoccupied with this question and wrote an extensive tract on the lessons of Hungary in which he arrived at the conclusion that intervention from Russia was just around the corner. He was turned down by the chief editors of four publications. Ultimately his prophetic tract was printed in the last, illegal issue of *Student* (Prague), on August 29, 1968, a week after the country had been invaded.[8]

Meanwhile, from the Soviet Union came ominous warnings that there the Czechoslovak developments were indeed closely compared to the antecedents of the Hungarian Revolution and the "proper" conclusions were being drawn. What particularly excited the Soviet leadership was the publication in *Literární Listy* (Prague) of Ludvík Vaculík's "2000 Words" manifesto on June 27,[9] which happened to be the anniversary of the journalists' debate sponsored by the Petőfi Circle in Hungary in 1956. This debate was a frontal assault on the Rákosi regime and led to the dismissal of the Hungarian party chief in the middle of July.[10] From the vantage of Moscow the parallel between the events in Budapest and Prague seemed striking and hardly accidental.

An editorial in *Pravda* (Moscow) over the pseudonymous author-
ship of I. Alexandrov (which stands for a collective product of the
paper's entire editorial board and thus ranks in importance just be-
low the level of unsigned editorials that come straight from the Politburo) reflected deep concern and explicitly linked Hungary and
Czechoslovakia:

> 'The 2,000 Words,' despite hypocritical phrases about 'defending'
> the interests of the Czechoslovak people, leaves no doubt as to the
> authors' real objectives. . . . Such tactics are not new. They were resort-
> ed to by the counterrrevolutionary elements in Hungary which in 1956
> sought to undermine the socialist achievements of the Hungarian people.
> Now, twelve years later, the tactics of those who would like to under-
> mine the foundations of socialism in Czechoslovakia are even more
> subtle and insidious. And the Czechoslovak working people, as well as
> all who hold dear the achievements of socialism, cannot fail to see the
> danger concealed behind the incitement to provocative activity urged
> by 'The 2,000 Words.'
>
> It has now become more obvious than ever that the appearance of 'The
> 2,000 Words' is not an isolated phenomenon but evidence of the increas-
> ing activity in Czechoslovakia of rightist and overtly counterrevolution-
> ary forces obviously linked with imperialist reaction. They have gone on
> to make fierce attacks against the foundations of socialist statehood.

To buttress his position, Alexandrov proceeded to quote excerpts from newspapers of fraternal parties:

> *Rabotnichesko Delo*, organ of the Central Committee of the Bul-
> garian Communist Party, notes: 'Attempts to undermine the party
> authority and eliminate its leading role and to destroy the people's
> unity as embodied in the National Front have now become fashion-
> able and widespread phenomena in Czechoslovakia. In point of fact,
> these attempts are designed to strike at the existing social system and
> push the country onto a dangerous, adventurist path.' . . .
>
> *Népszabadság*, organ of the Central Committee of the Hungarian
> Socialist Workers' Party, writes: 'We, too, lived through periods that
> were similar in many ways and know from our own experience the
> thoughts and intentions concealed behind the formulation of "The
> 2,000 Words." Those who are speaking out against the people's rule,
> against the socialist system and its legal order must be fought by the
> most effective means required in the present situation.'

To make sure that the meaning of his analysis was not lost on the
reader, Alexandrov ended his article by stating: "In the struggle for
the strengthening of socialism in Czechoslovakia and for friendship
among the peoples of the socialist states, the working class and all
the Czechoslovak working people can always count on the understanding and *complete support* [my italics] of the people of the
Soviet Union."[11]

The July issue of *Kommunist*, the Soviet Central Committee's theoretical monthly, carried an article couched in very similar terms by Pëtr N. Demichev, a Party secretary in charge of cultural and ideological affairs:

> Historical experience has shown that expectations concerning democracy and 'liberalization' are used by counterrevolutionaries as a smoke screen for attempts to liquidate the conquest of socialism and socialist democracy. We can recall how, during the Hungarian events of 1956, it was under these slogans that counterrevolution meted out bloody drumhead justice to communists.
>
> Therefore it is necessary to give a prompt and decisive rebuff to all attempts by imperialist apologists to slander the socialist state and socialist democracy.[12]

Procrustes had clearly spoken and by his measure the Czechoslovak reformers did not fit the bed. They would have to be cut down to size.

Although the thrust of Alexandrov's and Demichev's authoritative comments could hardly be mistaken (they bespoke intervention if it were needed), they fell on deaf ears in Czechoslovakia. The country's reformers simply would not admit that their case was in its fundamentals not different from that of Hungary, that evaluated by different standards (and not necessarily by those of Procrustes alone) it was possible to discover many structural similarities between the Hungarian events of 1956 and those in Czechoslovakia a dozen years later.

One cannot say what would have happened if the Czechoslovak reformers had been able to overcome what were essentially romantic and utopian notions of national distinctness and to apply cool, rational analysis to their situation. Would they have changed course to avoid head-on collision with the Soviet Union and its minions? Would they have been forearmed (in the literal sense of the word) to meet the eventuality of a Soviet onslaught? (The answer to this question is: Most likely not.) But, speculating about might-have-beens is useless. The point is that, regardless of the outcome, the Czechoslovak reformers would have been well advised to broaden the context of their analyses and draw inferences from the experiences of neighboring countries. It is difficult to see how a nation can passionately pursue universal ideals of humanist socialism and simultaneously remain estranged—or if not estranged, isolated—from its immediate environment. Either these ideals are universal, in which case they are shared or at least attainable by others as well, or they are particular to a given nation, in which event they may not be realizable because of the hostility of the international environment. Like it or not, the destinies of Czechoslovakia and Hungary are closely intertwined.

There was tangible evidence of this during the "Prague Spring" and not only in the commentaries of Soviet spokesmen. Alexander Dubček met János Kádár on three occasions, more than any other East Central European communist leader. Their first meeting in the Czechoslovak border town of Komárno took place on February 4, the second in Budapest on June 13 and the third, again in Komárno, on August 17. Kádár was the first and the last of the East Central European leaders seen by Dubček. What transpired between the two men is not known. Perhaps Kádár was acting in behalf of the Russians, precisely because of the applicability of the Hungarian situation to Czechoslovakia. Perhaps he warned Dubček about the trap threatening him. Richard Lowenthal suggests that Kádár may have met with Soviet leaders vacationing at Yalta to dissuade them from invasion.[13] Another source, a reasonably high-ranking functionary in the Press Department of the Soviet Central Committee, told me, years after the event, that it was Kádár's exasperated report about Dubček's absolute recalcitrance (following their meeting on August 17) that persuaded the Soviet leadership of the need to act expeditiously. One need not put too much stock in my informant's assertion. He had obvious and good reasons for shifting the blame away from the Soviet leadership. Yet, one wonders.

In any event one must hope that the lessons of 1968 will not be lost on the Czechoslovaks. After repeated historical disasters in a relatively short time span, it should be clear to them that it is perilous and perhaps even incorrect to draw sharp distinctions between their evolutionary pattern and that of their neighbors. For better or for worse, there is a community of fate between them and the surrounding socialist countries. Their best hope of achieving their ideals is in concert with these nations and not apart from them, regardless of fancied or real differences in national traditions, values, heroes, myths, economic structure and sociopolitical experiences.

NOTES

1. See, for example, Vladimir V. Kusin, *The Intellectual Origins of the Prague Spring* (New York, 1971), p. 153. This brilliant study, which traces the development of reformist ideas among the Czech intelligentsia from 1956 to 1967, makes no reference whatever to any influence the Hungarian Revolution might have had on the thinking of Czechoslovak reformers.

2. For materials on the Czechoslovak purge trials and commentary about the political scene in the 1950s, see Karel Kaplan, "Zamyšlení nad politickými procesy [Thoughts about the Political Trials]", *Nová mysl* [New Thought],

XXII (1968), No. 6, 785-794; No. 7, 906-940; No. 8, 1054-1078; also Jiří Pelikán (ed.), *The Czechoslovak Political Trials, 1950-1954* (Stanford, Calif., 1971), p. 360.

3. For an extensive analysis of the Czechoslovak regime's reactions to the Hungarian Revolution, see Pavel Tigrid, "Marx na Hradčanech" [Marx at Hradčany Castle], *Svědectví*, III, No. 11, 227-240.

4. Ibid., 240 ff.

5. V. Mencl and F. Ourednîk, "What Happened in January," *Život strany*, No. 16, 1968. Printed in Radio Free Europe, *Czechoslovak Press Survey*, No. 2142 (November 29, 1968), p. 22.

6. E. Goldstücker, "Let Us Talk About It, Friends," *Literární Listy*, May 16, 1968. Printed in Radio Free Europe, *Czechoslovak Press Survey*, No. 2086 (June 1968), pp. 2-3.

7. O. Machotka, "Takě Jedno Výročí," [Another Anniversary], *Literární Listy*, June 13, 1968.

8. I. Sviták, "Prologue to Intervention," *Student*, August 29, 1968. Printed in I. Sviták, *The Czechoslovak Experiment, 1968-1969* (New York, 1971), pp. 131-134.

9. L. Vaculîk, "2,000 Words to Workers, Farmers, Scientists, Artists, and Everyone," *Literární Listy*, June 27, 1968. Printed in R. Remington, (ed.), *Winter in Prague* (Boston, 1969), pp. 196-202.

10. See Paul E. Zinner (ed.), *National Communism and Popular Revolt in Eastern Europe* (New York, 1956), pp. 327-331, and Zinner, *Revolution in Hungary* (New York, 1962), p. 210.

11. I. Alexandrov, "Attack on the Socialist Foundations of Czechoslovakia," *Pravda*, July 11, 1968. Printed in Remington, *op. cit.*, pp. 203-207.

12. P. N. Demichev, "Building of Communism and the Social Sciences," *Kommunist*, July, 1968, pp. 14-35. Printed in Remington, *op. cit.*, pp. 208-212.

13. R. Lowenthal, "Sparrow in the Cage," *Problems of Communism*, XVII, No. 6 (November-December 1968), 2-11, 14-24.

PART III
THE REVOLUTION AND THE WEST

Stephen Borsody

IMRE NAGY AND EUROCOMMUNISM

To reverse the order of two key words in the famous first sentence of *The Communist Manifesto*: A specter is haunting communism—the specter of Europe.

The specter that is haunting Soviet communism today is called European or democratic communism—Eurocommunism for short. Its principal spokesmen are the Italian Enrico Berlinguer, the Spaniard Santiago Carrillo, and the Frenchman Georges Marchais. They are leaders of Western Europe's most significant communist parties, and what they are in effect saying is that they repudiate the tyrannical form of Soviet communism and submit to the rules of Western democracy. Should this Eurocommunism be in fact what it purports to be, it may well close the chasm that so tragically weakened the socialist movement in the West after the First World War, when Lenin launched his campaign against democratic socialism. It would certainly deliver the *coup de grâce* to Soviet leadership in the communist movement, including the Russians' claim to infallibility as the high priests of Marxist dogma.

Eurocommunism as a democratic form of government is still a theoretical proposition in the West, with opinions widely divided over whether its promise is a political trick or a sincere conversion. Within the Soviet orbit of power, however, on two notable occasions European communists in control of central government did act democratically in the Western sense of the term.

During the "Prague Spring" of 1968, the Czech communists started to behave like Western democrats, only to be struck down by Soviet arms even before their incipient, but unmistakably genuine, Eurocommunism could fully develop. In the other instance, however, during the fast-moving thirteen days of the Hungarian Revolution in 1956, from October 23 to November 4, democratic communism in the Eurocommunist sense did reach its full dimension. Imre Nagy, the communist prime minister of the Hungarian revolutionary regime, did exactly what the Eurocommunists say they will do if they come to power in a national government: Nagy followed the will of the people, he obeyed the rules of democracy.

Imre Nagy's conversion to democratic communism seemed to come in response to the demands of the revolution. Appointed prime minister by the Russians on October 24 to save the crumbling Soviet-imposed communist dictatorship in Hungary, Imre Nagy became the liquidator of that hated regime. On October 27, he named five noncommunists to the 28-member prerevolutionary communist cabinet. On October 30, at the glorious climax of the revolution, he hastily formed a new government, consisting of three communists and three noncommunists. Finally, on November 3, on the eve of the brutal Soviet armed attack on Budapest, he enlarged his government so that it had a 9:3 noncommunist majority, which reflected more accurately the size of the parties supporting Nagy.

The abolition of the communist one-party system was a return to a democratic coalition system, which Hungary had experienced after the free elections of 1945 and which was destroyed by the Soviet coup in 1947. In a significant departure from Hungary's political past, however, Nagy declared Hungary's neutrality on November 2, 1956, simultaneously withdrawing from the Warsaw Pact. The Hungarian people stood united behind these moves; there was no civil war situation. The revolution against Russian occupation and Soviet tyranny was triumphant for a moment under a communist premier—and so was Eurocommunism, in today's parlance.

Western critics as a rule see in Imre Nagy's policies during the revolution nothing but improvised responses to popular demands and pressures—patriotic actions at best, and precipitate ones at worst, provoking the Soviet reprisal that led to failure and tragedy. Not infrequently, Nagy is blamed for lack of political wisdom in "going too far." In these widely held views there is often a careless factual mistake concerning the chronology of events. The Soviet decision to invade Hungary with full force was, in fact, made before Nagy announced Hungary's withdrawal from the Warsaw Pact—and not the other way round. But even among the better-informed Western experts few seem to be familiar with Nagy's political ideas, which explain his actions. No wonder Nagy is simply marked down in Western

opinion as a national communist, no different from others who pop-
ped up at one time or another in East Central Europe to assert their
countries' or parties' independence from Soviet domination.

Nagy's actions during the revolution were not in fact improvised
and his motivation was not quite like that of the regular national
communists. All his moves and decisions were deeply rooted in his
rather unusual convictions, unusual in particular for a so-called
Muscovite communist, as he was by virtue of his long years of exile
in the Soviet Union. He formulated these views long before the
revolution of 1956. He collected them in the so-called dissertation
he submitted to the Central Committee of the Hungarian Workers'
Party in self-defense against his detractors after his dismissal as prime
minister in 1955.[1]

The curious thing about this "self-defense" is that Nagy's detractors, Mátyás Rákosi and his Muscovite clique who became Hungary's rulers under the Stalinist terror, were actually able to use it as
a proof of their charges against Nagy—namely, that he was anything
but a loyal communist in the Soviet Russian sense of the term. On
the other hand, poor as Nagy's dissertation was as a self-defense at
that time, it has great value as evidence of Nagy's extraordinary intellectual independence and courage as a communist thinker—
evidence above all that Imre Nagy was actually among the founders
of that communist ideology which has recently come to be known
as Eurocommunism.

It is nothing less than amazing (as amazing as the case of some of
the Soviet dissidents) that a communist who spent a good part of
his life in the Soviet Union should be able to create such a synthesis
of revolutionary communism and civilized Europeanism as Imre
Nagy did. This civilized Europeanism, and not just the Magyar patriotism which his Hungarian followers admire in him, accounts for
the remarkable ease with which the communist Nagy could assume
leadership of a national revolution against the communist regime
imposed by force on Hungary by the Soviet Union. For it should be
noted that, in addition to being national and anticommunist, the
Hungarian Revolution of 1956 was emphatically pro-European. Its
elemental force was fed to a very large degree by the Hungarians'
desire to be free from the perverse ties of the Soviet orbit and to be
reunited with Europe, whose culture and civilization the Hungarians,
throughout their checkered history, always proudly considered
themselves part of.

Imre Nagy has often been lumped together with the Tito type of
national communists. And national communist he was. But Nagy's

national communism was of a peculiar variety, as was, for that matter, the communist attitude toward nationalism in Soviet-dominated Hungary.

Basic to an understanding of this peculiarity is the fact that Hungary, alone among the nations in the Soviet orbit after the Second World War, was subject to a loss of territory at the Paris peace settlements of 1947, which left over one-fourth of the Hungarians under the foreign rule of neighboring countries. All the other Soviet-bloc nations, irrespective of their resistance records or the side they had taken in Hitler's war, were awarded some gains, either by means of population expulsions or territorial annexations or both. The Soviet Union itself joined Hungary's neighbors in mutilating Hungarian ethnic territory by annexing the formerly Czechoslovak-held Sub-carpathian Ruthenia along with its Hungarian population. Consequently all the communist parties indulged in the popular pleasures of ethnic-nationalist exaltation, cleverly reaping the dividends of popular satisfaction with national aggrandizements under communist auspices. The only exception was Hungary. There, the communist party denounced nationalism indiscriminately as a bourgeois deviation. In particular, the notion of Hungarian national unity in defiance of ethnic dismemberment was branded an unsavory legacy of the anti-Semitic "Fascist" past.

Unlike his Muscovite communist colleagues, Imre Nagy fully understood both the complexities and the absurdities of this situation. He tried to act as a conciliator. He did this with the spontaneous Hungarian national feeling of a peasant, as he was by origin, and without a trace of anti-Semitism toward his Jewish-born fellow communists who, by Moscow's cynical grace, ruled Hungary. To appease the anti-communist hostility of the individualistic Hungarians, Nagy worked toward a compromise between European democracy and Soviet communism. And, in order to heal the wounds of ethnic dismemberment, he dedicated himself to promoting reconciliation with Hungary's neighbors in the spirit of Danubian federalism.

Imre Nagy's indictment of Hungary's Moscow-appointed communist leadership is summed up in this characteristic sentence, written in January 1956, ten months before the revolution: "The inner tension in Hungary, which is chiefly political, is caused by the fact that the leadership is opposing the ideals of national independence, sovereignty and equality, as well as Hungarian national feeling and progressive traditions."[2] He called for the liquidation of every vestige of the "Stalinist autocratic rule."[3] But, unlike other so-called national

communists, Nagy's concern was not limited to a revision of relations between the Soviets and his own nation. He was also concerned
with the relations between East Central European and Western European communism. This is the typical Eurocommunist tenet in his
thinking. It reveals itself throughout his dissertation. Nagy's ideology was as different from the Soviet way of thinking as it was thoroughly European:

> The Soviet form and methods of building socialism, its mechanical
> application, disregarding the special characteristics of various individual
> countries, raise serious obstacles in the path of international revolution-
> ary workers' movements, primarily and especially to the work of the
> communist and workers' parties in the Western capitalist countries in
> *their* [his italics] battle for socialism. For Central and Eastern Euro-
> pean countries, and last but not least for us, it is necessary that we find
> and use such forms and methods in building socialism in all phases of
> social, political, economic and cultural life, and we must realize such a
> rate of progress that it will make socialism acceptable and desirable to
> the widest possible masses in the capitalist countries and to all strata of
> the working classes.
>
> Our social, economic and cultural situation, from which we proceed-
> ed to build socialism, is in many ways very close to the situation that
> prevails in the capitalist countries of the West. Therefore the similar-
> ities in the situations of the Western capitalist countries and the present
> people's democracies in Central and Eastern Europe make it possible
> that by the application of a creative Marxism-Leninism, taking into
> consideration the special character of the transition period and the situ-
> ation in various countries, as well as the new road to socialism, one can
> extend immeasurable aid to the communist and workers' parties of
> Western Europe in gaining the support of the working masses in their
> struggle for socialism. Our conspicuously proper or improper stand-
> point on principles, our good or our bad work, our success or our fail-
> ure, can promote or impede the cause of socialism in Western Europe.[5]

Imre Nagy's intense concern for East Central European communism's image in the eyes of Western Europe was quite unique. His belief in Western values placed him unequivocally in the company of
the Eurocommunists. It set him apart, too, from East Central European national communists who, while breaking away in one way or
another from the Soviet line, seldom embraced Western values. Rumania's national communist leader, Nicolae Ceauşescu, remains in
fact a true believer in the Soviet form of authoritarian communism
and Josip Tito of Yugoslavia, the prototype of national communism,
has made only superficial concessions to Western ways for the sake
of political expediency.

Throughout his dissertation, Imre Nagy backed up his views with
references to the "five principles" of the Bandung Conference of

1955, which were endorsed by the Soviet Union as well. But even while evoking the Bandung principles of national independence and sovereignty, territorial inviolability, nonaggression, noninterference in internal affairs, equality and peaceful coexistence, Nagy had no use for the notion current among so-called nonaligned communists, glorifying the non-Western world as a fountainhead of new ethics in politics. Nagy's mind was on Europe:

> The noble traditions of these five basic principles have roots in our country also, which were formed during our historic development. There were periods in history when the light of these principles and ideals of ours shone brightly in all of Europe. The noble traditions of battles for independence are still alive today, and have their effect, nurturing these principles as our greatest national virtue. Attaining national independence and sovereignty where it is nonexistent, or preserving it, has always been the greatest national problem in past periods, as it is today and will be in the future, even under the socialist system's development.[6]

In international affairs, Imre Nagy advocated the liquidation of power groups. He defended the right of "neutrality" against the power groups and called for cooperation among the "progressive democratic socialist" countries within the framework of "active coexistence" with "countries having a different system." As for his own country, Nagy emphatically declared: "It is the sovereign right of the Hungarian people to decide in which form they believe the most advantageous international status will be assured, and in which form they think that national independence, sovereignty, equality and peaceful development will be attained."[7]

He invoked the vision of "our great national genius" Lajos Kossuth, who "envisioned the assurance of an independent, sovereign, self-governing Hungary, not through alignment with a Great Power or through joining a power group, but by close cooperation with neighboring peoples within the framework of a federation of free and independent nations."[8]

Much like the ideas of Eurocommunists today, Imre Nagy's philosophy of communism in his day was totally at odds with the Soviet totalitarianism and Russian imperialist interpretation of Marxism-Leninism. But, unlike the Eurocommunists of the West, Nagy had to pay with his life for his deviation from the Soviet line. And the irony of Nagy's tragedy is that János Kádár, who rode to triumph over Nagy's dead body, was Nagy's close associate during the revolution of 1956, identifying himself with Nagy's views and actions. Under still unknown circumstances, Kádár defected to the Russians to form a pro-Soviet puppet government, while Nagy was captured by the Russians and executed almost two years later, in June 1958.

János Kádár, the traitor of 1956, proved to be a skillful compromiser in his dealings with the Russians. Despite Hungary's continued Russian occupation, Kádár had created possibly the most liberalized communist society within the Soviet orbit of power. But to say, as some people do, that under Kádár the Hungarians have achieved the objectives of their defeated revolution, is to forget that the Hungarians under Imre Nagy were fighting for an independent, sovereign, neutral, democratic socialist Hungary. It is also to forget that the desire to break away from the stifling Soviet bloc and to rejoin the open community of Europe was the great force behind the revolution of 1956—and also the force behind the prerevolutionary ferment, called the "purifying storm" by the communist writers who inspired it. Significantly, one of these writers, Tamás Aczél (novelist, one-time Stalin Literature Prize winner and a contributor to the present work), wrote a stirring poem entitled "An Ode to Europe."

The Soviets murdered millions. Among them was the Hungarian prime minister, Imre Nagy, the only head of government killed by the Russians in their East Central European satellite empire since the Second World War. Not too many people in the so-called free world know or remember the barbaric facts about Soviet Russian communism. President Gerald Ford's ignorance about Soviet domination in East Central Europe, revealed during the presidental campaign in 1976, is a case in point. Yet there is new hope. One reason not to despair of the free world's indifference to the cause of freedom is President Jimmy Carter's concern with human rights. Another is the welcome fact that at long last the leading communists of Western Europe are calling the Soviets' bluff of posing as leaders of progressive mankind. The Eurocommunists are drawing the line between their democratic communism and the tyranny of Soviet communism.

It may still be only a guess whether Western Eurocommunists in a national government would act as tyrants or as democrats. But there can be no mystery about how haunted the Soviets must feel by the voice of a Berlinguer, Marchais, or Carrillo. The kind of people who sent Imre Nagy, the martyr of Eurocommunism, and scores of others like him to their deaths are still the masters behind the walls of the Kremlin. When they look West toward Europe they must feel uncomfortable.

134   THE HUNGARIAN REVOLUTION IN RETROSPECT

NOTES

1. The English version: Imre Nagy, *On Communism: In Defense of the New Course* (New York, 1957; reprinted Westport, Conn., 1974).
2. Ibid., p. 40.
3. Ibid., p. 29.
4. Ibid., p. 14.
5. Ibid., pp. 9-10.
6. Ibid, pp. 23-24.
7. Ibid., p. 33.
8. Ibid., p. 34.

Péter Kende

WESTERN EUROPE

What effect did the Hungarian Revolution have on Western Europe? Did it, in fact, have any? After twenty years the answer is beginning to take shape, though, without research into primary sources, it must perforce be incomplete, hypothetical or impressionistic. The aftereffects of major events always pose a lot of knotty problems for historians, even if the lapse of several centuries has eliminated any possible bias. An unbiased approach to the history of Europe of the last two centuries is almost impossible to take. It is very hard to analyze even such episodes as the revolutions of 1848 or the Franco-Prussian War of 1870-1871 free of current preconceptions. How much more difficult it is, the,. to consider 1917! It was a prominent French historian, Pierre Vidal-Naquet, who recently observed that the average Frenchman's ideas about ancient Greece are easier to explain in terms of late eighteenth-century Jacobin democratic ideology than by means of contemporary Greek realities.

These preliminary comments are by way of forewarning that this essay can only be a personal synthesis, colored by the author's biases and hopes. The only objective elements will be the three planes of treatment of the impact of the Hungarian Revolution: the internal conflicts among Western political forces, the evolution of leftist ideologies and the prestige of Soviet communism.

* * *

Unquestionably, the main result of 1956 in Western European political life was the recession of communism and the spread of anticommunist public opinion. The ground for this had already been prepared by what had happened only a few years earlier, by the events of the latter half of the 1940s. Ruthless extinction of democratic political processes began in the Soviet zone of Europe in

Rumania and Yugoslavia in 1945 and continued in Hungary and Poland in 1947 and in Czechoslovakia in 1948. These suppressive measures earned the communist parties, dependent as they were on Moscow, a pestilential reputation in Western Europe, where they were
virtually shut out of national life. This vigorous anticommunism had
somewhat abated by the mid-1950s, when the new course that came
into existence after Stalin's death raised new hopes all over the
world. All the earlier anti-Stalinist "slanders" had been substantiated
by Nikita Khrushchev's revelations of Stalin's "mistakes and crimes"
and their exposure justified the belief that something was beginning
to change in the Soviet world after all.

The outcome of the Hungarian Revolution was worth a hundred
of Khrushchev's speeches. De-Stalinization had to do only with the
professional politicians, but the revolution burned itself into the
consciousness of everybody from the youngest to the oldest, for all
of whom it had the traumatic effect of watching powerlessly a tragedy at close hand. It was as much an event in the streets of Hungary
as it was in those of Paris, Copenhagen, Linz, Glasgow and the small-
est villages in Calabria. Over the years many of my friends here in
France, now thirty-five or forty, have confessed that the course of
the Hungarian Revolution brought home to them the meaning of
international fellowship. There were even families where the parents
and grandparents had their children pray for the Hungarians every
night.

Not since Adolf Hitler had there been such a telling illustration of
what imperialism really was. For today's generations it had been a
long time since there had been a straightforward, comprehensible
and effective demonstration of what really happens when a giant
Great Power, armed to the teeth, moves into a rebellious province to
drown a freedom movement in blood. The lesson was learned by everybody—almost everybody, regardless of his political or ideological
stripe. The few who did try to justify the Russians' actions were exposed to universal contempt and attracted the passionate scorn of
the man in the street, whose feelings were all the more inflamed by
his sense of impotence. The burning of communist party offices in
France was partly a conscious retaliation for what newsreels showed
was happening in Budapest and was partly an expression of general
public outrage at the events in Hungary. The point was not lost on
the French communists: to this day, twenty years later, they have
never again unblushingly called the Soviet aggression in Hungary
"liberation."

The Hungarian question plunged the communist parties of Western Europe into deep crisis. From Austria to Britain members quit by the thousands. The Danish Communist Party, which had not been insignificant before the Hungarian Revolution, ceased to exist to all intents and purposes, because its entire leadership élite, including Secretary General Aksel Larsen, abandoned it and formed the new and independent Socialist People's Party. The French Communist Party lost the majority of the intellectuals who had joined it during the Second World War. Its support among the electorate was badly eroded: in early 1956 it had received 5.5 million votes, 26 per cent of those cast; at the next election in the fall of 1958 it received only 3.9 million votes, 19 per cent of those cast. True, events in Algeria and the accession of Charles de Gaulle also contributed to this decline. The Italian Communist Party alone weathered the storm without major casualties. This was due to the policy of Palmiro Togliatti, who had already begun to keep a certain distance between himself and the Russians. Yet even in Italy the communists could not prevent their own isolation: their unity front with the socialists was shattered for good in 1956. It took more than a decade for the Western European communist parties to break out of the quarantine into which the events of that year thrust them.

It should be emphasized that the communists' isolation was moral as well as political. The forces of the moderate left, primarily the social democrats, drew practical conclusions from 1956 by breaking off all connection with the communists. A prerequisite of existence for the communists had been to belong to a so-called leftist unity front or at least to pursue an apparent dialog with the socialist parties. This was true wherever the communists existed politically—which was not the case in Great Britain and West Germany, of course. As a consequence of 1956 not only did the moderate socialists turn their backs on the communists but so did their fellow travelers. The Italian left-wing Socialist Party led by Pietro Nenni cut all ties with the communists. The French cryptocommunist "Progressivist" political group simply evaporated into thin air.

To read contemporary essays and press statements by the moderate left might lead one to believe that their decisions on the communists were final. In history, however, nothing is final, of course; interests usually supersede moral pledges. It is reserved to individuals for loyalty to principles to determine behavior, and even then not all the time. Political alliances follow the rigid logic of power. In France less than a decade and a half had to elapse before the communists' propositions for unity were to become attractive to the socialists again.

The political panorama cannot be complete without taking into account the Trotskyists, anarchists and others to the left of the communists. To anyone unfamiliar with the Marxist sectarians, it might come as a surprise to learn that for the extreme left 1956 was the start of a renaissance after a long period of torpor. The Trotskyists had been stubbornly insisting since the 1930s that the Soviet system was a betrayal of the socialist revolution. Year after year they had waited for the fulfillment of Leon Trotsky's prophesy that one day the working class would rise up against the "usurpers" of power. Yet, for reasons not necessary to elaborate, they had remained objects of ridicule everywhere. And lo, in 1956 the miracle happened after all. The uprising in Poznań and the nationwide events in Hungary in October were the eagerly awaited fulfillment of the prophesy. The national aspects of these events did not disturb the Trotskyists in the least. They were satisfied that at last somewhere on earth the working class had acted against the "bureaucrats" controlling the state, just as Trotsky's theory had predicted. Ever since, Hungary has been the Sacred Land to them. In their bulletins they never miss an opportunity to agitate for war against the bureaucrats on the model of the Hungarian Revolution.

*   *   *

The post-1956 renaissance in Trotskyist and anarchist trends, which reached their peak in the late 1960s, leads me to the problems of ideology. Let me say in advance that I intend to analyze only certain aspects of the evolution of leftist thought. The reasons for this limitation are only partly personal. It is clear, even without lengthy analysis, that events that occur within the communist world make far bigger waves in leftist than in conservative thinking. Among liberal thinkers, the most inspired by the Hungarian Revolution were those who really speak to the left, like Raymond Aron.

Without nationalist pretensions, 1956 can be said to have opened a new chapter in leftist systems of thought. The previous chapter had begun in 1917 and was brought to a close by 1956. Notwithstanding the bloodshed, betrayal, violence, failures and disappointments attendant upon the Leninist experiment in transforming society, its most signal result, the Soviet state power, remained the dominant theme of all branches of socialist thought, even if only for polemical reasons. The social democrats, for instance, would cite Soviet methods as the antithesis of the proper ones. The philosopher Jean-Paul Sartre considered Soviet practice, despite its imperfections, the realization of Hegelian-Marxist universal doctrine. It is astounding that such outstanding minds as Beatrice and Sidney Webb and H. G. Wells could regard the Soviet system as a tentative experiment that would lead to a new civilization. Stalin's deeds ought to have removed the scales from the eyes of all such observers but, for some mysterious reason, the Western intellectuals always reacted to the lies and violence of Soviet Russia not objectively but ideologically.

The Soviet tanks that trundled through Budapest in the fall of 1956 were expunging not only Hungarian liberties but also the ideal of Soviet socialism. To the background rumble of guns, the obsequies were impressive and, for Europe, final: never again will anyone exhume the corpse of Soviet socialism. It was its final Wagnerian thundering. The toppling statue of Stalin in Budapest's City Park brought the Soviet Valhalla down with it. The crude reality of the political and military infrastructure of state power was laid bare. The three Baltic states have been riveted to that framework for a long time; so have the Ukraine, Georgia and, for that matter, the whole Russian nation. Why is hard to say but ever since then the scene has not been the same. From that moment on, Soviet Russia ceased to be the Messiah of the proletarian revolution. Something had been sundered in leftist minds. Soviet power is now seen to be a classic embodiment of the oppressive gendarme; its role, rigid, banal, but hellish no longer.

At this point I must confess that the data available become defeatingly vast. From the German-American Herbert Marcuse to the Franco-Greek Cornelius Castoriadis, the leftists have consumed and produced such reams of ideological material as even to defy classification. Besides, it would be absurd to attribute everything that has happened since 1956 to a single, common cause. Nothing could be more alien to this writer than to try to create a new myth in which a Hungarian Messiah replaces the Soviet one. Yet it is worth noting that the historical peak that Eastern Europe reached between 1956 and 1968 posed new problems for Western European political thought. Foremost among these are the threat of totalitarian one-party rule and the matter of defense against it.

What is so new in all this, it might well be asked, particularly by anybody who still remembers the antitotalitarian writings of the 1950s. Has not everything there is to say about the Leninist-Stalinist state system in comparison with fascism already been said by Czesław Miłosz, Hannah Arendt, Raymond Aron, Carl J. Friedrich and Zbigniew Brzeziński? It is a fair question, except its implication that there is an absolute truth that can be enunciated once and for all.

From the standpoint of ideological purity, the liberals' criticism was substantial. But the Hungarian Revolution's "criticism by arms" (to use Karl Marx's felicitous phrase) opened a new avenue in leftist minds. The realities of East Central Europe inspired a new generation of theorists bred, for the most part, within the Marxist school. When the bubble of the totalitarian delusion burst, as a leading group of French neo-Catholic intellectuals put it in reference to what happened in Hungary, it put new life into so-called libertarian socialism.

The criticism of totalitarianism, including rejection of the centrally planned economy, brought liberal and socialist ideologies much closer together, though a definitive, constructive line has yet to emerge. Will the future be the "self-governing" model? Or will it be the fusion of small business and collective capitalism into a "market socialism"? Neither the Hungarian Revolution nor the Czechoslovak ferment of 1968 produced an answer. I am convinced that the search for new social patterns will be long. To expect an answer to be found in the next twenty or thirty years would be futile. Totalitarian Marxism is by no means a dead letter yet. It holds whole generations in Europe under its ideological sway and its intractable tenacity shows that the regeneration of social ideas is likely to be a very long drawn-out process.

The Hungarian Revolution set a precedent in the sphere of political action and for this has already been recognized as one of the great revolutions of Europe. Before 1968 both friends and foes could make common cause in condemning the Hungarians for trying to go too far and so inevitably provoking Soviet interdiction. This charge has been muted since the events in Prague. In fact, now both opponents and supporters see it as a virtue that the Hungarian Revolution clearly announced its political aims—pluralistic democracy and withdrawal from the Warsaw Pact, the goals the Hungarians took up arms for. According to French historians, the Hungarian Revolution compressed into its short span the whole cycle that it took the French Revolution in another century months, even years, to complete. With the passage of time, attention has come to be increasingly focused on the Workers' Councils of Budapest. They remained virtually the sole representatives of revolutionary legality after all armed resistance had been crushed and Imre Nagy's legally constituted government had been deported. At a scholarly conference held in Paris on the twentieth anniversary of the revolution, an interesting debate turned on whether the Workers' Councils had intended to play the same role as the soviets did in 1917. On the basis of documents from the Central Workers' Council of Budapest, a distinguished commentator, Claude Lefort, argued that the Hungarian Workers' Councils did not contemplate seizing full power but, on the contrary, were intent on the democratic separation of the economic and political spheres. This was the lesson they had drawn, Lefort said, from the parlous experience of Soviet totalitarian power.

To leftists, what the Hungarian workers did in the fall of 1956 lends decisive support to the contention that it is a fallacy to equate Soviet power with socialism or the defense of socialism. This view has been further borne out by the events in Czechoslovakia in 1968 and the Polish workers' demonstrations that keep on flaring up periodically. The first objective evidence for it was offered half a century ago by the Kronstadt revolt in 1920. But, as already noted, the ideological mills of the Marxist left grind very slowly. Besides, the memories of every generation have to be refreshed anew. In other words, Budapest reaffirmed Kronstadt and reasserted the workers' deeprooted demand for a council system without party control. On some Western socialists it has only just begun to dawn what the real issue is.

The one area where the heritage of the Hungarian Revolution has not received its just deserts is in understanding the principles and purposes of Imre Nagy. To an observer in Central or Eastern Europe, it is obvious that the ideological roots of the current Spanish, Italian and, to a lesser extent, French Eurocommunist experiments lie in Hungarian and Polish revisionism and their climax in 1956. Yet the "Prague Spring" is normally deemed their antecedent; Imre Nagy, however, was a far more resolute and conscious exponent of national sovereignty and "socialism with a human face" than ever Alexander Dubček. What is it about Nagy that unsettles his Western European successors? I think it is neither his personality nor even his ideas but an objective historical dilemma. Nagy was a communist and a friend of the Soviet Union to the bottom of his heart. He was driven to break with the Soviet Union by the part he played in the revolution— by his position, not by his intentions. Nagy could have avoided the rupture only if he had chosen to heed Soviet dictates rather than his countrymen. Western communists do not acknowledge the dramatic justice of Imre Nagy's actions and thus give us to understand that, in a similar predicament, they would opt for Moscow instead of their own nation.

*   *   *

The power of the Soviet empire in 1956 successfully halted and effectively stifled the first major insurrectionary outbreak to explode within its borders. Its action was facilitated by the fact that, apart from Poland, there was no opposition evident anywhere else, the West was in no position to take any steps, and the new trends under Khrushchev promised some improvement over the old madness under Stalin. It was the latter climate that made the compromise under János Kádár possible. The consolidation of Soviet control was also expedited by happenstance. The launching of the first sputnik in 1957, a few months after the Hungarian crisis, created a new situation for the Soviet Union, restoring its international prestige far more rapidly than its leaders could ever have hoped at the end of 1956. The empire's political stability (as distinct from economic conditions, which are quite another story) was further enhanced by favorable changes in the global balance of military power.

The Soviet victory in November 1956 was nevertheless Pyrrhic. Moscow was able to crush the East Central European insurrection only by resorting to the most traditional methods of imperialism, including brazen military assault, overt violence and arrant violation of the principles the Soviet Union championed in normal times of peace. These tainted the Soviet image indelibly. In the broadest sectors of popular public opinion, Russia has once again been turned back from the defender of revolutions into a reactionary great power, "the prison of nations." Budapest has laid a string of time bombs that keep on blowing up. One detonated not long ago in Portugal and another has done so even more recently among the Western European communists.

The long-term effects are apparently being felt more and more. Reading the European leftist press is particularly instructive in this regard. European public opinion has become more unanimously negative toward Soviet socialism than at any time in the past sixty years. The Soviet Union in the 1970s is the exemplar for none. It would be an exaggeration to attribute all this to 1956: at least two other factors have contributed to it. One is the running Czechoslovak sore; the other, the new Russian émigrés. The open hostilities against the Soviet Union which were renewed in 1968 led to the "normalization" of Prague, which has done nothing to ease matters—nor has its manifest failure. The other, more important factor has been the messages coming out of Russia. Once more it is being shown that a handful of courageous men can do more than God knows how many divisions, men like Pëtr Grigorenko, Aleksandr Solzhenitsyn, Vladimir

Bukovskiy. Ever since the publication of Solzhenitsyn's major work, "Gulag" has become synonymous with the Soviet political system. It is no jest to say that the only support offered the Hungarian insurgents has come from this new Russian "heavy artillery."

It is very hard to recreate history with the wisdom of hindsight, but let us try.

It is widely held that the Moscow leadership intervened in the Hungarian Revolution by force of arms to forestall internal disintegration, but were there only two possible alternatives: disintegration or military aggression? It is a known fact that domestic reform had been on the minds of the Soviet leaders ever since 1953. One objective alternative would have been to turn the communist bloc into a looser form of commonwealth, the members of which would have owed Moscow political loyalty but not ideological conformity. If this had been done, not only would the Soviet Union have been spared its catastrophic "victory" in Budapest but also Poland would have had a chance at renaissance, the Prague Spring would probably have occurred ten years earlier and the positive effects of all these would have radiated back into the Soviet Union itself. Is this a utopian vision? It was Khrushchev himself who proposed a model for a freer "socialist commonwealth." Even more to the point is the fact that this is precisely what he introduced in the form of the new relationship between the Soviet Union and Yugoslavia. The essence of Imre Nagy's political vision was to extend the same principle to Hungary. The Moscow leadership, in ruthlessly suppressing the Hungarian Revolution, demonstrated its utter inability to reform its empire.

This was the trigger of the start of the decline of Soviet communism in 1956. The process may last decades, but one thing is certain: it has begun. The elderly demidictators who personify the system are obviously the last generation of a state structure that is ossified, terrified of change and so becoming more and more of an anachronism. This system is threatened by dissent and schismatic tendencies in its western marches. It is even more seriously imperiled by the surfacing and growth of centrifugal forces fed by the passions of the nationalism in its central regions.

This essay has not dealt with the economic problems of the Soviet world, although, if there is any area where the reputation of the Soviet system is lower than in the political sphere, it is the economic. There is no longer any question that the bureaucratic planned economy is static, technically backward and creature to unrelenting problems in the production of consumer goods. Expert opinion varies only on the extent of the failure. It is worth noting that the economic experts of East Central Europe have an even more jaded opinion of the Soviet economy than their Western counterparts. A political economist in Budapest or Warsaw can only chuckle when he reads the estimates of the Soviet economy published by the Joint Economic Committee of the U.S. Congress. Soviet prestige is unassailed in just one area—military power. In all others it is in shreds. The man in the street regards Russia with pity; the left seeking its utopia looks on in anger; the Western communists are simply embarrassed. For now, it is hard to imagine that the Soviet Union can reverse its decline without radical changes.

In view of the Soviet Union's direct impact on Hungary and its neighbors, this assessment is not very encouraging. But in historical perspective, the chance these nations have to take action is as open as the fact that the decay of the Soviet empire dates from its "victory" over them is obvious.

THE UNITED STATES

It was a dramatic moment indeed!

On November 1, 1956, at 10:26 a.m. a teleprinter on the twentieth floor of the United Nations headquarters building in New York suddenly tapped out:

—*United Nations New York are you there?*

—*Yes we are still here.*

The operator answered readily, a little surprised, and then found from his code book that the caller, Diplomag Budapest, was the Hungarian foreign ministry.

Ordinarily a message from a member nation is conveyed by its official delegation, but at that time the revolutionary government of Hungary had no official delegate at the United Nations. Besides, that Thursday was to turn out to be the most fateful day of the revolution.

All day long Prime Minister Imre Nagy had been urging the Soviet ambassador in Budapest, Yuri Andropov, to explain the massive troop movements taking place in the northeastern part of the country. Finally, realizing that Andropov was misleading him, the prime minister, with the approval of the reorganized communist party leadership and the revolutionary coalition government, had repudiated the Warsaw Treaty and declared Hungary neutral.

The teleprinter message, which had come from Budapest to Vienna by landline, then to New York by radio, continued:

—*If you are busy, I call you later.*

The answer was genial:

—*We are not busy, can wait if you want.*

The exchange of banalities kept the line open for two hours. Then at 12:21 p.m. came a message addressed to Secretary General Dag Hammarskjöld:

—I request Your Excellency promptly to put on the agenda of the forthcoming General Assembly of the United Nations the question of Hungary's neutrality and the defense of this neutrality by the four Great Powers. Signed: Imre Nagy, President of the Council of Ministers of the Hungarian People's Republic, designated Minister of Foreign Affairs.

The desperate appeal disappeared into a huge pile of papers on the desk of the United Nations secretary general, who was out to lunch.

It was only under persistent questioning by journalists quoting European sources on Hungary's declaration of neutrality that the United Nations press chief salvaged the message and read it to reporters at 2 p.m.

A perplexed world followed the events in Hungary, the fighting in the streets of Budapest, with admiration and sympathy. Demonstrations against the Soviet Union were staged in many cities.

Political action was concentrated at the United Nations, where all the attempts to counter what was happening were lost in an impenetrable tangle of goodwill, hesitation, ambiguity, incompetence, hypocrisy and hostility.

It looked like conspiratorial timing but it was, I believe, simply ominous historical coincidence that Britain, France and Israel should have launched their attack on Egypt on October 29, 1956. The Suez conflict put a different perspective on the world, setting friends and allies against each other and providing the Russians with the opportunity and excuse they needed. The United Nations was preoccupied with Suez and the ensuing confusion was an invitation to the Soviet government to move easily, forcefully and brutally against Hungary.

When Imre Nagy's message was officially circulated, delegates began speculating what was meant by "forthcoming session." An uncaring or unfriendly interpretation would point to the regular fall meeting, the Eleventh Session, which had been interrupted by the emergency session on Suez. But with a little goodwill and understanding, Imre Nagy's words could just as well be taken as a crucially important and very urgent request for Hungary to be added to the emergency session's agenda.

The teleprinter line remained open all day. A clarification could have been obtained very easily.

The Security Council had already held an urgent meeting to consider events in Hungary at the request of Britain, France and the United States on October 28, the eve of the Suez landings. A Soviet agent named Lev Konduktorov, posing as Dr. Péter Kós, "permanent

Hungarian delegate to the United Nations," had vehemently protested against the council meeting as "a violation of Hungary's sovereignty."

By a vote of nine to one (the Soviet Union against and Yugoslavia abstaining), however, the Security Council had resolved to place an item , "The Situation in Hungary," on its agenda.

Three days later, on November 1 at 5:00 p.m., the General Assembly opened its bitter emergency session on Suez. The United States was allied with the Soviet Union against Britain, France and Israel—strange bedfellows, to be sure. The name of Hungary came up logically when a British diplomat contrasted the action in Egypt with the Soviet Union's armed intervention in Hungary. Hungary was mentioned again at the end of the session when an Italian diplomat called the delegates' attention to what was happening there, but no concrete steps or moves were proposed.

When United States Secretary of State John Foster Dulles mounted the tribune at 7:00 p.m., his first words raised some hopes: "I doubt that any representative ever spoke from this rostrum with as heavy a heart as I have brought here tonight." But it was not Hungary that had made Dulles's heart heavy. In fact, he did not mention Hungary at all. What made him so despondent was the vote he was about to cast against Britain, France and Israel.

As a matter of fact, while campaigning in Dallas on October 29 for President Dwight Eisenhower's reelection, Dulles had emphatically declared that Washington did not regard the new governments of Poland and Hungary as potential military allies. Eisenhower himself, while praising the Hungarians for their brave fight for freedom, had made the same point in a television broadcast. No one had sought military aid or suggested any alliance between Hungary or East Central Europe and the West, but the American secretary of state, who saw morality as the prime motivating force in foreign policy, had instructed Charles Bohlen, the American ambassador in Moscow, to draw the Soviet leaders' attention to these two statements. Nikita Khrushchev and the Soviet government could hardly have wished for a more unequivocal green light. They drew the correct conclusion!

Hungary's fate was sealed. In the early hours of November 4, the mighty Soviet onslaught was unleashed. In New York it was nearly midnight, November 3. In the United Nations General Assembly's continuing emergency session on Suez, the American chief delegate, Ambassador Henry Cabot Lodge, was recognized on a point of order and informed the hushed chamber that Budapest was under heavy bombardment.

Within three hours—by which time it was already 10:00 a.m. on November 4 in Budapest—the Security Council had been called to order, but a United States draft resolution to look into the Hungarian state of affairs was defeated by a Soviet veto. Nevertheless, by invoking the "Uniting for Peace" resolution, the council managed to bypass the Soviet veto and voted by ten to one to call an emergency session of the General Assembly "to make appropriate recommendations concerning the situation in Hungary."

At emergency sessions of the General Assembly held between November 4 and 9 and at meetings of its regular Eleventh Session between November 19 and December 12, a series of resolutions was adopted—calling for a cease-fire, condemning the Soviet Union for brutal military intervention, requiring the withdrawal of Soviet troops from Hungary and granting the Hungarians free elections. At the same time Secretary General Dag Hammarskjöld made repeated efforts to gain admission to Hungary, but without success.

When time for the General Assembly's regular session ran out on January 10, 1957, a special committee was set up to investigate the situation "created by the intervention of the Soviet Union, through its use of armed forces and other means, in the internal affairs of Hungary in order to report its findings to the General Assembly."[1]

The committee interviewed 111 witnesses, all of whom had left Hungary after the suppression of the revolution. Two hundred petitions were reviewed and information was gathered from various governments. The committee even tried to go to Hungary and to visit Imre Nagy in exile in Rumania.

The committee's conclusions are already history. The uprising had been spontaneous. The revolutionary councils and the government had come into being on the initiative of the Hungarian people. The revolution had its roots in the Hungarians' past and was inspired by their traditional love of freedom. It was the Russians who had provoked events, even to the point of constraining Nagy to withdraw Hungary from the Warsaw Pact and declare its neutrality.

The report, a clear, concise 148-page document, was presented to the General Assembly with the unanimous agreement of the committee.[2] After long and impassioned debate, the resolution recommended by the committee was passed on September 14, 1957, by sixty votes to ten with ten abstentions.[3] The resolution:

> *Notes* the conclusion of the Committee that the events which took place in Hungary in October and November 1956 constituted a spontaneous national uprising.

Finds that the conclusion reached by the Committee on the basis of its examination of all available evidence confirms that:

(a) The Union of Soviet Socialist Republics, in violation of the Charter of the United Nations, has deprived Hungary of its liberty and political independence and the Hungarian people of the exercise of their fundamental human rights;

(b) The present Hungarian regime has been imposed on the Hungarian people by the armed intervention of the Union of Soviet Socialist Republics;

(c) The Union of Soviet Socialist Republics has carried out mass deportations of Hungarian citizens to the Union of Soviet Socialist Republics;

(d) The Union of Soviet Socialist Republics has violated its obligations under the Geneva Convention of 1949;

(e) The present authorities in Hungary have violated the human rights and freedoms granted by the Treaty of Peace with Hungary; return to Hungary of those Hungarian citizens who have been deported to the Union of Soviet Socialist Republics.

Reiterates its concern with the continued plight of the Hungarian people;

Considers that further efforts must be made to achieve the objectives of the United Nations in regard to Hungary in accordance with the Purposes and Principles of the Charter and the pertinent resolutions of the General Assembly;

Calls upon the Union of Soviet Socialist Republics and the present authorities in Hungary, in view of evidence in the report, to desist from repressive measures against the Hungarian people, to respect the liberty and political independence of Hungary and the Hungarian people's enjoyment of fundamental human rights and freedoms, and to ensure the return to Hungary of those Hungarian citizens who have been deported to the Union of Soviet Socialist Republics;

On the evening of June 17, 1957, Radio Budapest announced the execution of Imre Nagy, General Pál Maléter and two of their associates. The Thirteenth Session of the General Assembly placed the Hungarian question on its agenda once more. After a solemn debate on December 11 and 12, 1958, a strongly worded resolution was adopted, censuring the communist regime of Hungary and the Soviet Union for the barbarous murders and for continuing violation of human rights. The assembly appointed Sir Leslie Munro of New Zealand a special representative and requested the USSR and the "present authorities of Hungary" to cooperate with him in the performance of his mandate. Needless to say, they never did cooperate but Sir Leslie's report on conditions in Hungary became a yearly feature of assembly sessions. Another annual exercise was the Credentials' Committee's recommendation to the assembly to "take no decision regarding the credentials submitted on behalf of the representative of Hungary."

The last shots were fired over Hungary at the United Nations in the early 1960s. On December 20, 1962, by a substantial majority the General Assembly reaffirmed its earlier resolutions, including its request for the withdrawal of Soviet troops from Hungary and assurance of the Hungarian people's fundamental rights, freedom and independence. It also resolved that its special representative was no longer needful and asked the secretary general to take "any initiative that he deems helpful in relation to the Hungarian question." The vote was 53 to 13 with 43 abstentions. Twelve members were absent.

The credentials of the representatives of the new government in Budapest were finally accepted by the assembly on January 8, 1963. Their acceptance was received with jubilation in the nonfree world and sadness by Hungarians. A small nation's hopes for justice and freedom had been destroyed. Why and how did this finally happen?

Secretary General Hammarskjöld made a revealing statement to the Danish Students' Association in Copenhagen in 1958: "In the Hungarian crisis, the United Nations confined itself to an 'expression of principle.' With the exception of one or two of the smaller countries, no one in the United Nations urged measures going further than those which were taken."

Maybe responsibility lies with the United States, but President Eisenhower vindicated himself and his country in a television interview with Walter Cronkite on November 23, 1961:

> There was no European country, and indeed, I don't believe ours, ready to say that we should have gone into this thing at once and tried to liberate Hungary from communist influence. I don't believe that we had the support of the UN to go in and make this a full-out war. We had no government [in Hungary] that was asking us to come in and it wasn't until there was a sort of, I think, a very brief revolutionary government was set up, that we had any communication with them. So I don't know.[4]

The last word belongs to Robert Murphy, undersecretary of state at the time of the Hungarian Revolution, who wrote in his memoirs:[5] "Perhaps history will demonstrate that the free world could have intervened to give the Hungarians the liberty they sought, but none of us in the State Department had the skill or the imagination to devise a way."

An honest assessment.

NOTES

1. The committee comprised Alsing Andersen (Denmark), chairman; K.C.O. Shann (Australia), rapporteur; R.S.S. Gunewardene (Ceylon [now Sri Lanka]), Mongi Slim (Tunisia) and Enrique Rodríguez Fabregat (Uruguay), members.

2. United Nations, *Report of the Special Committee on the Problem of Hungary* (New York, 1957).

3. It may be instructive to see how the vote broke down:

For:

Argentina	France	Morocco
Australia	Ghana	Netherlands
Austria	Greece	New Zealand
Belgium	Guatemala	Nicaragua
Brazil	Haiti	Norway
Britain	Honduras	Pakistan
Bolivia	Iceland	Panama
Burma	Iran	Paraguay
Cambodia	Iraq	Peru
Canada	Ireland	Philippines
Chile	Israel	Portugal
China (Taiwan)	Italy	Spain
Colombia	Japan	Sudan
Costa Rica	Jordan	Sweden
Cuba	Laos	Thailand
Denmark	Lebanon	Tunisia
Dominican Republic	Liberia	Turkey
Ecuador	Libya	United States
El Salvador	Luxemburg	Uruguay
Ethiopia	Mexico	Venezuela

Against

Albania	Czechoslovakia	Rumania
Bulgaria	Hungary	Ukraine
Byelorussia	Poland	USSR
		Yugoslavia

Abstaining

Afghanistan	Finland	Saudi Arabia
Ceylon (Sri Lanka)	India	Syria
Egypt	Indonesia	Yemen

4. Tranmitted by Columbia Broadcasting System Television (Channel 2), November 23, 1961.

5. *Diplomat Among Warriors* (New York, 1964).

THE CONTRIBUTORS

TAMÁS ACZÉL, D. Lit., is Professor of English, University of Massachusetts, Amherst. A leading intellectual, he was a member of Imre Nagy's circle both before and during the revolution of 1956. Author (with Tibor Méray) *The Revolt of the Mind: A Case History of Intellectual Resistance behind the Iron Curtain* (New York, 1959); *The Ice Age* (New York, 1965). Editor: *Ten Years After: The Hungarian Revolution in the Perspective of History* (New York, 1966). Coeditor: *Poetry from the Russian Underground* (New York, 1973).

ANDREY A. AMALRIK is a writer and lecturer at the State University of Utrecht. Author: *Prosushchestvuyet li Sovetskiy soyuz do 1984 goda?* [Will the Soviet Union Survive until 1984?] (Amsterdam, 1969); *Nezhelannoye puteshestviye v Sibir* [Involuntary Journey to Siberia] (New York, 1970).

STEPHEN BORSODY, J.U.Dr., is Emeritus Professor of History, Chatham College, Pittsburgh. He was a diplomat and journalist in Hungary. J.U.Dr., Charles University, Prague; Privatdocent in East European history, University of Budapest. Author: *The Triumph of Tyranny: The Nazi and Soviet Conquests of Central Europe* (New York, 1960); *The Tragedy of Central Europe* (New York, 1962). Contributor: *The Development of Historiography*, ed. Matthew A. Fitzsimons et al. (Harrisburg, Pa., 1954); *Czechoslovakia Past and Present*, ed. Miloslav Rechcigl (The Hague, 1969); *The Austrian Empire: Abortive Federation?*, ed. Harold J. Gordon, Jr., & Nancy M. Gordon (Lexington, Mass., 1974).

ADAM BROMKE, Ph.D., is Chairman, Department of Political Science, McMaster University, Hamilton, Ont., and President, International Committee for Soviet and East European Studies. M.A., St. Andrew's University; Ph.D., University of Montreal and McGill University, Montreal. Author: *Poland's Politics: Idealism vs. Realism*

(Cambridge, Mass., 1967). Editor: *The Communist States at the Crossroads* (New York, 1965). Coeditor: *The Communist States and the West* (New York, 1969); *The Communist States in Disarray* (Minneapolis, 1972); *Gierek's Poland* (New York, 1973).

STEPHEN FISCHER-GALAŢI, Ph.D., is Professor of History, University of Colorado, Boulder, and Editor, *East European Quarterly*. A.B., A.M., Ph.D., Harvard University. Author: *Ottoman Imperialism and German Protestantism, 1521-1555* (Cambridge, Mass., 1959); *The New Rumania: From People's Democracy to Socialist Republic* (Boston, 1967); *Twentieth Century Rumania* (New York, 1970), and others.

GEORGE G. HELTAI, Dr.Jur., Dr.R.Pol., is Professor of History, College of Charleston, S. C. He was a member of Imre Nagy's circle; Deputy Minister of Foreign Affairs in Imre Nagy's government in 1956. He was Director, Imre Nagy Institute of Political Science, Brussels, and Editor of the institute's journals, *The Review: An International Quarterly* and *Études*, from 1959 to 1963.

PAUL JÓNÁS, Ph.D., is Professor of Economics, University of New Mexico, Albuquerque. Dr.ŒEc., University of Technical and Economic Sciences, Budapest; Ph.D., Columbia University. Author: *Projections and Forecasts for the Indian Economy* (New Delhi, 1959); *Taxation of Western Enterprise in Selected Socialist Countries* (Washington, D.C., 1976); "The Gerschenkron Effect: A Re-Examination," *Review of Economics and Statistics*, February 1970; "Production Index Bias as a Measure of Economic Development," *Oxford Economic Papers*, December 1970; "Soviet Growth in Absence of Centralized Planning," *Journal of Political Economy*, March-April 1974.

PÉTER KENDE, Ph.D., is Research Professor of Economic Sociology, Centre National de la Recherche Scientifique, Paris. Ph.D., University of Paris. Author: *Logique de l'économie centralisée* (Paris, 1964); *L'Abondance est-elle possible?* (Paris, 1971). Contributor: *Encyclopédie de la sociologie: Le présent en question* (Paris, 1975). Coeditor: *Selected Essays on the Hungarian and Polish Events of 1956* (Paris, 1977).

ANNA KÉTHLY (1889-1976) was Minister of State in Imre Nagy's government of 1956. A Member of the Hungarian Parliament from 1922 and Secretary General of the Social Democratic Party of

Hungary, she was purged and imprisoned after her party was merged in 1948 with the Hungarian Communist Party to form the Hungarian Workers' Party. During the Hungarian Revolution she reorganized the Social Democratic Party of Hungary. She attended the Socialist International meeting in Vienna on November 1, 1956, and was prevented from returning to Hungary by the Soviet intervention there three days later.

BÉLA K. KIRÁLY, Ph.D., is Professor of History, Brooklyn College and Graduate School, City University of New York. In 1956 with the rank of Major General, he was Commander in Chief, National Guard of Hungary; Commandant of Budapest; and Chairman, Revolutionary Council of National Defense. B.A., Ludovika Military Academy; M.A., War (General Staff) Academy, Budapest; Ph.D., Columbia University. Author: *Hungary in the Late Eighteenth Century: The Decline of Enlightened Despotism* (New York, 1969); *Ferenc Deák* (Boston, 1971). Editor: *Tolerance and Movements of Religious Dissent in Eastern Europe* (Boulder, Colo., 1975); *The Habsburg Empire in World War I* (Boulder, Colo., 1976); *East Central European Perceptions of Early America* (Lisse, The Netherlands, 1977).

GEORGE KLEIN, Ph.D., is Professor of Political Science and Chairman, European Studies Program, Western Michigan University, Kalamazoo. B.A., M.A., Ph.D., University of Illinois. Author: "Yugoslavia: The Process of Democratization" in Peter A. Toma (ed.), *The Changing Face of Communism in Eastern Europe* (Tempe, Ariz., 1970); "The United States and Yugoslavia" in Chester L. Hunt and Lewis Walker (eds.), *Ethnic Dynamics* (Homewood, Ill., 1974); "Detente and Czechoslovakia" in Peter J. Potichnyj and Jane P. Shapiro (eds.), *From Cold War to Detente* (New York, 1976).

IMRE KOVÁCS is a free-lance writer. He was a member of a group of populist writers calling for a radical reform in Hungary before the Second World War and his first book, *A néma forradalom* [The Silent Revolution] (Budapest, 1937), earned him three months in prison. He was consequently expelled from the University of Economics, Budapest, before finishing his studies and banned from all other Hungarian universities. He was Secretary General of the Hungarian National Peasant Party, 1939-1946, and a Member of the Hungarian Parliament, 1945-1947. He left Hungary in November 1947, just before the communist takeover, and settled in the U.S.A., where he became a Senior Editor for the Free Europe Committee and President of the International Center for Social Research. Author: *A Kivándorlás* [Emigration] (Budapest, 1938); *A parasztéletforma csődje* [The Bankruptcy of the Peasant Way of Life] (Budapest, 1940); *Magyar feudalizmus—Magyar parasztság* [Hungarian Feudalism—Hungarian Peasantry] (Budapest, 1941); *Szovjet-Oroszország agrárpolitikaja* [The Agrarian Policy of the Soviet Union] (Budapest, 1943); *Elsüllyedt ország* [The Sunken Country] (Budapest, 1945); *Agrárpolitikai feladatok* [Problems of Agrarian Policy] (Budapest, 1946); *Im Schatten der Sowjets* (Zürich, 1948); *D'une occupation à l'autre: La tragédie hongroise* (Paris, 1949); *The Hungarian People's Republic* (New York, 1951); *An Enquiry into the Agrarian Problems of Latin America* (New York, 1962). Editor: *Facts about Hungary: The Fight for Freedom* (New York, 1958).

JÓZSEF KŐVÁGÓ, LL.D., is a Senior Research Engineer. During the Hungarian Revolution he was elected Secretary General of the Smallholders' Party and Mayor of Budapest and was a member of the Imre Nagy government's delegation to the Warsaw Treaty Organization. B.S., Bolyai Academy; M.S., University of Technical and Economic Sciences, Budapest; M.A., War (General Staff) Academy, Budapest; LL.D. (honoris causa). Author: *Budapest on the Threshold of the Winter, 1945-1946* (Budapest, 1945); *Budapest on the Road to Revival* (Budapest, 1946); *You Are All Alone* (New York, 1959).

TIBOR MÉRAY is the Editor of *Irodalmi Újság* [Literary Gazette], Paris, and Vice-President, P.E.N. Club in Exile (French Section). On the staff of *Szabad Nép* [Free People], official daily of the Hungarian Workers' Party, from 1946 to 1955, he was its Korean and Chinese correspondent in 1951-1953. A close associate of Imre Nagy, he was Secretary and Party Secretary of the Hungarian Writers' Association, a principal of the "Writers' Revolt," a leading speaker at the Petőfi Circle and a member of the Revolutionary Council of Hungarian Intellectuals. Diploma in Hungarian and Latin literature, University of Budapest; winner of the Kossuth Prize and twice winner of the Attila József Prize. Author: *Thirteen Days That Shook the Kremlin* (New York, 1959); (with Tamás Aczél) *The Revolt of the Mind: A Case History of Intellectual Resistance behind the Iron Curtain* (New York, 1959); *La rupture Moscou-Pékin* (Paris, 1966); *That Day in Budapest* (New York, 1969).

IMRE NAGY (1896-1958) was twice Prime Minister of Hungary and led the Hungarian Revolution of 1956. Professor of economics at Karl Marx University of Economic Sciences, Budapest. Author:*On Communism: In Defense of the New Course* (New York, 1957), a collection of his essays published in several languages.

G. HUGH N. SETON-WATSON, D.Litt., is Professor of Russian History, University of London; Fellow of the British Academy; and Member of the Council, Royal Institute of International Affairs, London. B.A., M.A., D.Litt., Oxford University. Author: *Eastern Europe between the Wars, 1918-1941(* (Cambridge, 1946); *The East European Revolution* (London, 1950); *The Decline of Imperial Russia, 1855-1914* (London, 1952); *The Pattern of Communist Revolution: A Historical Analysis* (London, 1953); *Neither War nor Peace: The Struggle for Power in the Postwar World* (New York, 1960); *The Russian Empire, 1801-1917* (Oxford, 1967). Coeditor: *R. W. Seton-Watson and the Yugoslavs: Correspondence, 1906-1941* (forthcoming).

PAUL E. ZINNER, Ph.D., is Professor of Political Science, University of California, Davis. B.S., Tufts University, Medford, Mass.; M.A., Ph.D., Harvard University. Author: *Revolution in Hungary* (New York, 1962); *Communist Strategy and Tactics in Czechoslovakia, 1918-1948* (New York, 1963). Editor: *National Communism and Popular Revolt in Eastern Europe* (New York, 1956).

EAST EUROPEAN MONOGRAPHS

1. *Political Ideas and the Enlightenment in the Romanian Principalities, 1750-1831.* By Vlad Georgescu. 1971.
2. *America, Italy and the Birth of Yugoslavia, 1917-1919.* By Dragan R. Zivojinovic. 1972.
3. *Jewish Nobles and Geniuses in Modern Hungary.* By William O. McCagg, Jr. 1972.
4. *Mixail Soloxov in Yugoslavia: Reception and Literary Impact.* By Robert F. Price. 1973.
5. *The Historical and Nationalist Thought of Nicolae Iorga.* By William O. Oldson. 1973.
6. *Guide to Polish Libraries and Archives.* By Richard C. Lewandski. 1974.
7. *Vienna Broadcasts to Slovakia, 1938-1939: A Case Study in Subversion.* By Henry Delfiner. 1974.
8. *The 1917 Revolution in Latvia.* By Andrew Ezergailis. 1974.
9. *The Ukraine in the United Nations Organization: A Study in Soviet Foreign Policy, 1944-1950.* By Konstantin Sawczuk. 1975.
10. *The Bosnian Church: A New Interpretation.* By John V.A. Fine, Jr. 1975.
11. *Intellectual and Social Developments in the Habsburg Empire from Maria Theresa to World War I.* Edited by Stanley B. Winters and Joseph Held. 1975.
12. *Ljudevit Gaj and the Illyrian Movement.* By Elinor Murray Despalatovic. 1975.
13. *Tolerance and Movements of Religious Dissent in Eastern Europe.* Edited by Bela K. Kiraly. 1975.
14. *The Parish Republic: Hlinka's Slovak People's Party, 1939-1945.* By Yeshayahu Jelinek. 1976.
15. *The Russian Annexation of Bessarabia, 1774-1828.* By George F. Jewsbury. 1976.
16. *Modern Hungarian Historiography.* By Steven Bela Vardy. 1976.
17. *Values and Community in Multi-National Yugoslavia.* By Gary K. Bertsch. 1976.
18. *The Greek Socialist Movement and the First World War: The Road to Unity.* By George B. Leon. 1976.
19. *The Radical Left in the Hungarian Revolution of 1848.* By Laszlo Deme. 1976.
20. *Hungary between Wilson and Lenin: The Hungarian Revolution of 1918-1919 and the Big Three.* By Peter Pastor. 1976.
21. *The Crises of France's East Central European Diplomacy, 1933-1938.* By Anthony J. Komjathy. 1976.
22. *Polish Politics and National Reform, 1775-1788.* By Daniel Stone. 1976.
23. *The Habsburg Empire in World War I.* Robert A. Kann, Bela K. Kiraly, and Paula S. Fichtner, eds. 1977.
24. *The Slovenes and Yugoslavism, 1890-1914.* By Carole Rogel. 1977.
25. *German-Hungarian Relations and the Swabian Problem.* By Thomas Spira. 1977.
26. *The Metamorphosis of a Social Class in Hungary During the Reign of Young Franz Joseph.* By Peter I. Hidas. 1977.
27. *Tax Reform in Eighteenth Century Lombardy.* By Daniel M. Klang. 1977.
28. *Tradition versus Revolution: Russia and the Balkans in 1917.* By Robert H. Johnston. 1977.
29. *Winter Into Spring: The Czechoslovak Press and the Reform Movement 1963-1968.* By Frank L. Kaplan. 1977.
30. *The Catholic Church and the Soviet Government, 1939-1949.* By Denis J. Dunn, 1977.
31. *The Hungarian Labor Service System, 1939-1945.* By Randolph L. Braham. 1977.
32. *Consciousness and History: Nationalist Critics of Greek Society 1897-1914.* By Gerasimos Augustinos. 1977.
33. *Emigration in Polish Social and Political Thought, 1870-1914.* By Benjamin P. Murdzek. 1977.
34. *Serbian Poetry and Milutin Bojic.* By Mihailo Dordevic. 1977.
35. *The Baranya Dispute: Diplomacy in the Vortex of Ideologies, 1919-1921.* By Leslie C. Tihany. 1978.
36. *The United States in Prague, 1945-1948.* By Walter Ullmann. 1978.
37. *Rush to the Alps: The Evolution of Vacationing in Switzerland.* By Paul P. Bernard. 1978.
38. *Transportation in Eastern Europe: Empirical Findings.* By Bogdan Mieczkowski. 1978.
39. *The Polish Underground State: A Guide to the Underground, 1939-1945.* By Stefan Korbonski. 1978.
40. *The Hungarian Revolution of 1956 in Retrospect.* Edited by Bela K. Kiraly and Paul Jonas. 1978.